dear Cia —
Enjoy the exploration of
learning with all these
wonderful museums &
the people you will meet —
Bonnie Pitman
1999

PRESENCE OF MIND:
Museums and the Spirit of Learning

Edited by Bonnie Pitman

Cover and chapter openings: Ohio Valley China Co., *Centerpiece*, 1893 (detail). Philadelphia Museum of Art: Gift of the Ohio Valley China Company.

Library of Congress Cataloging-in-Publication Data

Presence of mind : museums and the spirit of learning / edited by
  Bonnie Pitman.
        p.   cm.
   Includes bibliographical references and index.
   ISBN 0-931201-58-6
   1. Museums--Educational aspects--United States. 2. Museums--
   United States--History. 3. United States--History--20th century.
I. Pitman-Gelles, Bonnie. II. American Association of Museums.
AM11.P74 1999
069'.0973--dc21   98-53146
                                                    CIP

PRESENCE OF MIND:
Museums and the Spirit of Learning

Edited by Bonnie Pitman

ACKNOWLEDGMENTS

The AAM Education Committee has been honoring individuals for their contributions to the museum education field for more than 15 years. The publication of *Presence of Mind: Museums and the Spirit of Learning* provides an opportunity to pay tribute to all of them. This book of first-person essays introduces the reader to individuals who have contributed both to museum visitors' quality of learning and the profession itself over the years.

I must first acknowledge the 17 colleagues and friends who authored the book's essays, advancing their ideas and beliefs about the issues that museums face. Their thoughtful and divergent essays illustrate the intelligence and breadth of thinking in our community. I also wish to thank the chairs of EdCom and the many professionals from various types of museums around the country who gave generously of their time to serve the committee and ensure its success. I particularly acknowledge Viki Sand and Mary Ellen Munley, who were the chairs of EdCom during the preparation of *Presence of Mind*.

A special tribute is due to all AAM presidents, now chairs, who have endorsed and supported EdCom since its founding in 1973. Notable among the presidents for their passion and commitment to promoting museums as educational institutions are Joel Bloom and Dan Monroe. Over the years, AAM's staff have also played a critical role. Edward H. Able, Jr., AAM's president and CEO, has been a steadfast advocate for the committee. Patricia Williams, vice president, policy and programs, and Kim Igoe, director, programs for museum advancement and excellence, deserve special mention, for I have called on them countless times for advice and counsel.

My mother, Margaret Perry, inspired my love of art and museums, and we have shared many visits to museums over the years. My son, David Gelles, has always supported my work, most recently the writing and editing of *Presence of Mind* during his senior year in high school. From his days in a stroller visiting the Metropolitan Museum of Art to our recent wanderings through museums in London and San Francisco, David has taught me to see and helped me to learn. His passion for museums has been a gift we share.   *Bonnie Pitman*

TABLE OF CONTENTS

TABLE OF CONTENTS

INTRODUCTION

by Bonnie Pitman

A nniversaries are times to reflect, celebrate, and look forward. Nineteen ninety-eight marked the 25th anniversary of the AAM Education Committee (EdCom), created on June 6, 1973, at the AAM annual meeting in Milwaukee. Recently, the current leadership and some of the committee's original members gathered to determine appropriate ways to celebrate EdCom's contributions to the field. *Presence of Mind: Museums and the Spirit of Learning* is the result of one recommendation—to invite the recipients of EdCom's John Cotton Dana Award for Leadership and Award for Excellence in Practice to contribute essays on the museum education profession. But first, some history.

EdCom was formed at a time when educators' voices were rarely heard at AAM meetings. During one session at the Milwaukee meeting, Linda Sweet, then at the Brooklyn Museum of Art and currently a partner with Management Consultants to the Arts, articulated a frustration common to museum educators. She observed that educators were often treated like second-class citizens within their museums, and that AAM annual meetings did not include programs of interest to the professionals and volunteers who worked with the public. Sweet urged those interested in addressing the issue to stay after the session. More then half the delegates did so, and a lively discussion and strategy session followed.

Individuals at that gathering created an ad hoc education committee and attempted to gather support from professionals working in art, history, science, and natural history museums, as well as the six regions represented by AAM. The group prepared a series of recommendations to be presented to delegates at the Milwaukee meeting:

> The Assembled Museum Educators at this convention have elected an ad hoc committee of 13 members to represent them. This Committee consists of both professional and volunteer educators geographically representing all museums in general, according to the AAM Bylaws (Chapter 3, Section 1). This ad hoc committee has met and respectfully requests that:
>
> *1.* The function of museum education be specifically represented on the AAM Executive Council by a member of the ad hoc committee or one of their alternates.
>
> *2.* This ad hoc committee be recognized as a presidentially appointed committee (Article 6, Section 3 of the AAM Constitution).
>
> *3.* Museum education, per se, be considered as a separate function regularly represented in program planning, publications, regional and national meetings.
>
> *4.* AAM establish, as soon as possible, a staff position to work with the ad hoc committee in implementing these aims.

Those who were present still remember the debate that followed. I remember that Harry Parker, deputy director for education at the Metropolitan Museum of Art, and Michael Spock of the Children's Museum, Boston, were among the many who urged support for the recognition of museum education professionals and their particular concerns. The resolution passed, with the exception of item four, and the ad hoc committee became the President's Education Committee of the AAM.

In those early years, EdCom focused on the role of the museum educators within their institutions, particularly their parity with curators and increasing their involvement in the planning of exhibitions. Some museum educators—though certainly not all—felt that their work with the public was outside the primary domain of the museum, which focused on the care and exhibition of the collections. In subsequent years, more education-focused programs were presented at the annual meetings of the regional and AAM conferences. Educators were elected to the AAM Council. Issues relating to museum educators and the interests of the public gained an increased presence regionally and nationally and continue to be seen in the EdCom's work today.

The publication of *Presence of Mind: Museums and the Spirit of Learning* is a tribute to the thousands of individuals who have contributed to working with the public. This includes a broad range of museum professionals and volunteers, and EdCom has long recognized their commitment to the field. In 1983, the Education Committee decided to recognize individuals who have made significant contributions to the profession with the Award for Excellence in Practice. Over the years, 16 professionals from art, history, natural history, children's, and science museums, as well as zoos, have been presented with this honor at the committee's annual meeting. In 1988, the committee determined that an award also should be given to individuals who have greatly influenced the work of the museum education field. In 10 years, only four individuals have received the John Cotton Dana Award for Leadership. Finally, in 1995, the committee began to honor institutions for their creative work in programs with the EdCom Awards for Excellence in Programming.

I invited the recipients of the Award for Excellence in Practice and the four recipients of the John Cotton Dana Award to contribute essays to what would become *Presence of Mind: Museums and the Spirit of Learning*. Only two winners of the Awards for Excellence in Practice are not represented in the book: Joan Madden, former chief, Office of Education, National Museum of Natural History, who retired in 1987, and Malcolm Arth, chairman of the education department, American Museum of Natural History, who passed away in 1991. Both Joan and

Malcolm were founding members of the Education Committee and contributed greatly in the early years of its work. Of the four individuals who received the John Cotton Dana Award—Michael Spock, Joel Bloom, Marlene Chambers, and Diane Frankel—only Joel was not able to contribute to the publication. While the voices of these three individuals are missed, I dedicate this publication to them in honor of their important role as mentors and supporters of museum education.

Except for Malcolm, the recipients of the Award for Excellence in Practice all have been women. This is a clear indicator of the role women have played in museum education. Seven continue to work in museum education—Tessa Bridal, Sally Duensing, Susan Bass Marcus, Barbara Moore, Mary Ellen Munley, Danielle Rice, and Patterson B. Williams. Alberta Sebolt George and I have become museum directors. Two recipients, Susan Bernstein and Elaine Heumann Gurian, are now consultants. And four have retired—Carolyn P. Blackmon, Zora Martin Felton, Joan Madden, and Judith White. The authors offer personal and professional reflections and discuss such issues as the role of museums and museum education in society; the unique ways in which museums educate; how the lack of funding and influence can affect work and relationships with the community; the importance and complexity of engaging multiple voices in the museum; and the dynamic influence of new technologies.

The framework for *Presence of Mind* evolved from a series of discussions with the award recipients and John Strand, director of AAM's publications department. We decided to present the authors with two questions:

1. What do you see as the two or three critical issues facing professionals working today to make museums effective educational institutions?

2. Whom are you learning from today; where or what are the future directions and sources of your ideas?

Each author responded to these questions in different ways, highlighting issues of audience, technology, community access and involvement, philanthropy, leadership, and teamwork. These essays do not suggest that education should be a greater priority than conservation, collections, or exhibitions. In fact, the authors recognize that aligning these aspects of museum work with the public dimension is critical. The essays in *Presence of Mind* are arranged in chronological order, based on the dates the awards were received. In the end the book is similar to a series of conversations with this distinguished group. The essays are reflections and also anticipate changes for the future.

At their best, museums are universal educational institutions of impressive scope, power, and authority. Through museums, people of varied backgrounds, education, ages, and cultures can experience the natural world and expand their understanding of what it is to be human. The recognition that the educational mission is part of every museum activity has dramatically affected the ways museums involve and support their communities. Today, museums are considered significant community assets, places that stimulate curiosity and enrich creativity through exploration.

Museums will continue, of course, to preserve the collections held in the public trust and to serve as centers for learning and engagement. Many of the *Presence of Mind* authors agree that museums also will continue to develop new relationships with their communities. An important trend I see is that museums are moving from a series of isolated initiatives to a unified voice for improvements in education, as well as social and economic reform. Collaborations at the local, regional, and national level will become increasingly important as individuals, museums, libraries, schools of arts and sciences, and other education organizations work to form a stronger fabric that defines our communities. These changes will center on improving the quality of the museum experience for the public that we serve. Focusing on policy and identifying new resources will occupy much of the work that we do in the new century. The opportunities for increasing the impact museums have locally and nationally are enormous. The valuable work of thousands of museum educators over the past quarter century has prepared us now to craft and enduring vision for the future, one in which museums can truly embody the spirit of learning.

AAM EDUCATION COMMITTEE
AWARD RECIPIENTS

AWARD FOR EXCELLENCE IN PRACTICE

1983   Bonnie Pitman, Deputy Director
       Seattle Art Museum

1984   Elaine Heumann Gurian, Special Assistant to the Secretary
       Smithsonian Institution, Washington, D.C.

1985   Joan Madden, Director of Education
       National Museum of Natural History, Smithsonian Institution,
       Washington, D.C.

1986   Malcolm Arth, Chairman, Department of Education
       American Museum of Natural History, New York

1987   Albert Sebolt George, Executive Vice President
       Old Sturbridge Village, Sturbridge, Mass.

1988   Danielle Rice, Curator of Education
       Philadelphia Museum of Art

1989   Judith White, Curator of Education
       National Zoological Park, Smithsonian Institution,
       Washington, D.C.

1990   Patterson B. Williams, Dean of Education
       Denver Art Museum

1991   Zora Martin Felton, Assistant Director
Anacostia Museum, Smithsonian Institution, Washington, D.C.

1992   Carolyn P. Blackmon, Chair, Department of Education
The Field Museum of Natural History, Chicago

1993   Sally Duensing, Assistant Director
The Exploratorium, San Francisco

1994   Tessa Bridal, Director, Theater Department
Science Museum of Minnesota, Saint Paul

1995   Susan Bass Marcus, Educator
Spertus Museum, Chicago

1996   Susan Bernstein, Education Coordinator
San Diego Museum of Man

1997   Barbara Moore, Head, Department of Education Publications
National Gallery of Art, Washington, D.C.

1998   Mary Ellen Munley, Director of Education and Outreach
Programs
The Field Museum, Chicago

JOHN COTTON DANA AWARD FOR LEADERSHIP

1988   Michael Spock, Director
                The Children's Museum, Boston

1991   Joel Bloom, Director
                Franklin Institute Science Museum, Philadelphia

1996   Marlene Chambers, Director, Publications
                Denver Art Museum

1998   Diane Frankel, Director
                Institute of Museum and Library Services, Washington, D.C.

The institutional affiliation for recipients of the Award for Excellence in Practice and the John Cotton Dana Award reflects where the person worked at the time the award was presented.

AWARD FOR EXCELLENCE IN PROGRAMMING

1995   Brooklyn Botanic Garden
                Project Green Research

1996   Brooklyn Children's Museum
                Museum Team

1997   Bruce Museum, Greenwich, Conn.
                Neighborhood Collaborative

1998   Philadelphia Museum of Art
                Family Rainbow

THE AAM EDUCATION COMMITTEE: MISSION AND GOALS

EdCom is the official Standing Professional Committee on Museum Education of the American Association of Museums. Founded in 1973, EdCom's purposes are: to promote high professional standards for museum educators; to increase the quality of communication among museum educators; to advocate for the support of museums and their educational purpose; to promote excellence in museum learning; to ensure that the concerns and needs of museum education are well represented in the policies, decisions, and programs of AAM on both national and regional levels.

STANDARDS. New members receive *A Statement of Professional Standards for Museum Education*, written and published by EdCom. Annual awards at national and regional professional levels recognize excellence in practice, programming, and leadership.

ADVOCACY. EdCom supports the advocacy efforts of AAM that affect national education policy. Museum education issues within AAM are represented through participation by EdCom members on councils and committees, including the Standing Professional Committee Council, AAM Strategic Planning Committee, Nominations Committee, and National Program Committee.

COMMUNICATION. Though regional and national newsletters, support for museum education Internet contact, and a system of state representatives, EdCom works to provide members with access to current issues, programs of interest, and advocacy initiatives.

SERVICES AND PRODUCTS. Program development for AAM national and regional meetings, the EdCom Members Directory, Marketplaces of Ideas, and publications, including the statement of professional standards and *Museums: Places of Learning*, provide EdCom members with resources to improve professional practice and to better serve museum audiences.

PLACES FOR
EXPLORATIONS AND MEMORIES

by Bonnie Pitman

S tanding directly in front of me was a little girl with a dark blue velvet dress, her golden curls held with a red bow. Surrounded by red, pink, and white flowers, she held a small watering can. The experience of looking at her soft face and the rich colors of her dress is riveted in my mind, as is the name of the artist, Pierre Auguste Renoir. I was 11 years of age, holding my mother's hand in the National Gallery of Art. It was clear to me then that I wanted to spend my life in museums. The idea that I could be in such a place, with art that could inspire awe and completely enthrall me, captivated my mind and directed my life.

During that summer our family also visited museums at the Smithsonian, Colonial Williamsburg, Fort Sumter, and Saint Augustine. My belief that museums are magical places where all members of a family can enjoy themselves and learn— separately or together—was clearly formed. My younger brothers stood on top of forts, scouting for war ships and aiming through gun holes at attacking armies. They were endlessly fascinated by displays of guns and swords. Meanwhile, I wandered through the rooms of old houses, engrossed in fantasies about the people who lived there hundreds of years ago. I did not need a story, facts, or a guide to help me. The fireplaces were filled with pots of hot food, long dresses rustled with each footstep, and I imagined the house filled with people and their conversations.

I collected every brochure and postcard available and pasted them into notebooks, creating my own museum of memories.

These experiences and images created the idea that museums were powerful places for discovery, imagination, and memories. I learned about history and art, and developed an awareness of and respect for other cultures. Because I am dyslexic, reading is not my preferred method for learning. Instead, I observe, touch, listen, imagine, and create. I was successful in museums where I was not successful in school. A door had opened to learning and understanding the world around me, and I rushed through it.

Along with many educators, I joined the museum profession in the early '70s, when there was a mandate to increase the educational role of museums. It was a time when individuals affected changes throughout the museum profession. At the Anacostia Neighborhood Museum in Washington, D.C., John Kinard pushed the walls of the Smithsonian into the neighborhood and helped to gain acknowledgment for the idea that all museums across the country have a social responsibility to their communities. Frank Oppenheimer opened the Exploratorium in San Francisco, where we learned about our senses through experiments in a place that was more like Merlin's cave than a traditional museum. Institutions like the Science Museum of Minnesota and the New Orleans Museum of Art began utilizing theater techniques as part of their interpretative programs, bringing ideas, people, and objects to life. Interactive exhibitions answering questions about daily life, such as how toilets worked, how many shapes bubbles can make, and what can be found in your grandmother's attic, were created at the Children's Museum in Boston by Michael Spock and his colleagues. New leaders in the field emerged to help create a wide range of initiatives that were broadly supported across the country.

The landmark report, *Museums for a New Century*, was published in 1984. This document and the resulting conversations and meetings shifted attention to the important educational role of museums and valued it along with the care and presentation of the collections. *Museums for a New Century* also raised awareness about the changes in the audiences museums served and the potential of new technologies. The educational role of museums was moved to the forefront as museums prepared for the next century. Joel Bloom, then director of the Franklin Institute in Philadelphia, was the co-chair for *Museums for a New Century*, and later became the president of the American Association of Museums. During his tenure at AAM, he formed a committee to prepare a policy statement on education and access in museums. I was invited to chair that committee, and we anticipated that our work would take approximately nine months. In the end the committee worked for two and a half years on *Excellence and Equity: Education and the Public Dimension of Museums*. This document went through 42 drafts and resulted in the first town meetings at the AAM annual meetings. The dialogue about the educational role of museums was now center stage. Everyone had opinions and concerns.

AAM's adoption of *Excellence and Equity* was considered a major achievement. This 25-page report that outlined issues to be addressed by museums and their communities was published in 1992. The recommendations ranged from a discussion about the central role of museums as educational institutions, with the responsibility for public service shared by the entire staff and board, to a call for increased leadership and financial support. Today, the museum field continues to be influenced by the recommendations in the report. *Excellence and Equity* has been broadly disseminated and has affected the way staff are trained and how staff and boards conduct their planning. Foundations, corporations, and federal agencies have increased their funding to support museum initiatives that address public access and education.

In the intervening years AAM, the Association of Science-Technology Centers, the Association of Youth Museums, and other professional organizations have developed a distinguished list of publications and technical documents about museum education, exhibitions, and marketing that have helped inform the field. The AAM Accreditation Commission revised its self study and assessment process to address the public dimension of museums and to encourage every institution to address these issues through its mission and allocation of resources. The commission also developed standards for museums to meet in their efforts to increase public services in all aspects of their planning, programs, exhibitions, marketing, research, use of the collections, and, of course, technology. In achieving these goals, the commission reflects the changes museums are making to respond to and influence their communities and to ensure their financial security. These initiatives speak to the need to both achieve excellence and sustain the future of the museum. It would have been impossible to predict that so many results would spring directly from one document, but clearly the stage had been set. Museums are recognized as centers for public learning for everyone, regardless of race, age, background, experience, or knowledge. Museums are forums and gathering places within communities, playing an increasingly important role in our changing society.

LOOKING AHEAD

The opportunities available to museums as we focus on education are countless and complex. Two that I have selected to comment on are rooted in my love of museums, my experiences with *Excellence and Equity*, my service on the AAM Accreditation Commission, and my work in art and children's museums. First, the physical spaces of museums impact the experiences visitors have; and, second, museums should increase our understanding about our primary audience—families.

Museums are extraordinary places for learning, experiencing, and engaging with ideas and objects. Museums are places where a person's natural curiosity can take root and expand. Museums provide a physical place for the encounter, bringing people and animate and inanimate objects together. We know that the experience of visiting a museum is very different from holding a book in your hands, searching for information on a computer screen, or watching a television. Exploration in a museum is rarely a linear progression; it is a collage of sounds and motion, rich in textures, sights, and smells—the contrasts of the cool or sometimes warm air, various levels of light, different qualities of floor surfaces; the varying scale of the architecture and the objects. Museums provide visitors with labels, maps, videos, publications, interpretive staff, and programs to help connect the images and ideas with the context and content of the subject matter that is being presented. Each visitor brings his or her own experience, knowledge, and feelings about art, history, and the sciences to his or her visit. The goal is to help visitors develop personal meaning through their interaction with the information and ideas presented by an object or in an exhibit. This is a complex interaction.

Museum experiences are site specific. The physical nature of the museum experience has a great deal to do with how visitors engage in learning. Museums rarely provide sequenced, didactic learning experiences like schools. Visitors wander until they decide to stop, attend, and engage—to learn about shelter, biodiversity, or an artist from South America. Visitors may enter cool halls of marble with imposing columns, seeing filtered light and hearing a fountain. They may encounter a dusty 18th-century village or come upon a small pathway in a moist and fragrant butterfly garden. The multiple dimensions of the museum experience go beyond the physical attributes of the architecture or landscaping of the space. At their best, museums create a place where people are comfortable and willing to explore new ideas while they encounter both the new and the familiar and use their senses and imagination to make connections and learn.

As educators, I believe we have undervalued the impact of the physical environment on our visitors. We attend primarily to visual learning experiences. Typically, designers focus on the proximity and lighting of objects in cases and on the walls, the point size and number of words on the label, and the content of what people see and read. In truth, we are missing the enormous potential of engaging visitors through the use of all of our senses—hearing, taste, touch, sight, and smell. Research developed over the last 25 years on learning and intelligence strongly indicates that museums should fully explore the full potential of the collections and physical qualities of the environment. Museums need to be more aware of the impact that sensory learning has on visitors. The senses of smell, touch, and taste are potent and often have greater impact on our long-term memory than sight. Living history museums like Old Sturbridge Village encourage visitors to look at and listen to the blacksmith as they smell the smoke of the coal fire, smell and taste the freshly baked cookies, and see and touch hand-woven wool. Visitors are given countless ways to create memories of the place; these engagements are designed to develop connections to people's daily lives. As we move forward, I believe museums would benefit from greater use of sensory learning when designing the facilities and programs.

SOCIAL AND FAMILY LEARNING

A major part of the museum learning experience is social interaction. The relationships among our visitors often provide a framework for their conversations, patterns of use, and level of knowledge. Visitors primarily come in groups, often with family members or friends. The individuals in the group may be experts or novices. We need to focus our research on the fact that the majority of our visitors come with another person to experience and enjoy our museums.

As our communities have changed, so should the traditional notion of a family audience. Families are composed of many different groups and types of people. The family group may include a husband and wife or sister and brother. They may come with their siblings or children, with relatives of various ages and relationships, or with friends. The family can also be caregivers with children or elderly relatives. Statistics show that family groups make up the majority of our museum visitors.

Why is it important to address families as our primary audience? I believe we need to examine the learning of family social groups in museums just as anthropologists study new communities. Rather than considering merely how one visitor learns about the objects being presented, museum educators, curators, and researchers should study how individuals in a group learn. Focusing on family learning also helps define the informal nature of museum learning and distinguishes museums from schools that provide formal learning experiences.

Most visitor experiences are situational and occur through social exchanges. Our visitors come as much for enjoyment, study, and education as for the opportunity to share new experiences with others. Because museums both educate and entertain, visitors hope that everyone in their group will both engage in learning and enjoy their time together.

The growth in tourism is a major trend that is affecting museums and the role of family groups. Cultural tourism is particularly important as research studies have found that even though families may make infrequent use of their own local museums, they will visit museums when they travel. These families would not consider their out-of-town visit complete unless they went to the museums, historic sites, and parks. These excursions are a type of pilgrimage to see the icons of our culture and reconnect with important events, people, and places of the past.

Museums play another important role in family life by offering a safe place to learn and play. The Bay Area Discovery Museum's focus groups with parents revealed specific information about how families use our site. Parents described how their children are not allowed to play in streets or at playgrounds without careful supervision due to concerns for safety. Today, children's lives are increasingly managed. They go in the family car from soccer games to music lessons and then to a friend's house; rarely are they allowed to wander the streets, to explore wild places on their own. Parents value the Bay Area Discovery Museum as a place where children can meet and interact with their peers. Parents described the museum as a safe place for these encounters and for social learning to occur.

The boys and girls in our focus groups described their experiences at the Discovery Museum of pretending to load fish onto a herring boat and then "selling" them at Fishermen's Wharf. Here, they worked with other children whom they had not met before. We know that social interaction is a critical part of the learning process for young children. It provides opportunities to observe and imitate the behavior of older children, learn to solve problems, and resolve differences. The museum is a place for this type of social learning to safely occur.

Museums would benefit from continued research and exploration on family learning. A number of excellent researchers have been documenting family learning in science museums. Similar studies are needed in other types of museums. Also, consider the fact that each year museums spend millions of dollars and resources on teacher training and school programs. While this is an important investment, there is another, even larger audience that is often underserved by museums—parents and families.

There are few places in our communities that educate individuals of different ages, learning styles, physical and emotional abilities, and levels of knowledge. Yet, each family includes such a broad range of people. Museums should seize this opportunity to engage families and do a much better job of supporting adults in their roles as teachers and learners. Museums often organize "family festivals," which gather a broad audience of children and adults. The festivals are fun and educational, but they should not be the only family services museums offer. Some museums have also developed a range of programs that involve parents in working and learning with their children on field trips, hikes, and classes. A focus on family programs represents a strategy for audience development that will require assessments of the museum's programs, publications, marketing, and positioning, but will undoubtedly strengthen its role in the community.

LAST THOUGHTS

Over the years I have applied a framework for the museum experience that I learned from reading Alfred North Whitehead, who defines the three stages of learning as "romance, precision and generalization" in his book *The Aims of Education*. In my translation of Whitehead's framework, in museums, "romance" means the enticement of the viewer with the wonder of the dinosaur, the mummy, or the Monet. It is the heady moment of seduction that draws you in and makes you want to see and understand more. The "romance" stage of learning is the process of discovery, curiosity, and exploration. It includes the moments of trying things out, looking at a subject for the first time, and celebrating the new and the different.

"Precision" is the next stage, in which the learner gathers information and absorbs it based on its relevance. This can occur through careful looking, reading labels, listening to a tour or lecture, or comparing objects that are arranged in the exhibition. Precision is the analytical phase of learning in museums, in which ideas become understood. It is the acquisition of information that discloses ideas with possibilities of significance.

"Generalization" is the stage in which the learner can translate new ideas and knowledge and place them in context. It is the stage of synthesis that allows museum learners to organize information into a framework or combine it with new information and create new knowledge and meaning. It occurs when the learner creates personal meaning from what she has learned, forming new understanding or discoveries about herself and/or the world.

We know that people learn best from experiences that they enjoy. The integration of education with entertainment and multiple forms of communication have made museums livelier places than those I visited as a young girl. We still provide moments of quiet reflection while also offering in opportunities for others to explore and engage together. The engagement of a broader public over the years has pushed the doors open for more people to enjoy museums as places where memories are formed.

THINKING ABOUT
MY MUSEUM JOURNEY

by Elaine Heumann Gurian

When I was young in the museum profession during the '60s and '70s, working in Boston, first at Summerthing, then at the Institute of Contemporary Art, and finally—for 16 years—at the Children's Museum, I believed that these institutions were like all others.

I worried then about access for all, especially for the novice learner, the shy, the anxious, and those who believed (because of their immigrant parents, their economic status, or their previously sheltered life experience) that when they entered a museum, they had come to the wrong place, a place that did not value them, make any allowance for what they did not know, or offer them images to which they could intuitively relate. I wrote, then, about welcome and love, experimented with hands-on and hands-off exhibition techniques, and talked about enfranchising visitors. I wished to make sure they felt not only welcome but refreshed by the experience.

I still believe in the value of these things but, 30 years past the '60s, I understand that the three institutions of my early career were rare communes of Nirvana. Never again in all my years of exciting museum work have these adventurous places been equaled in their humanity, their commitment to idealism, or their ease in transforming dreams into action. Only the Exploratorium during those same years seems in the least similar. I and all my early colleagues felt lucky to be where we were, doing what we did. Because we were given the chance, we collectively created places that valued everyone and nurtured ourselves. Young people in Boston in the '60s (and we were all young then!) believed in the effectiveness of social action, the value of love, and the courage of the naive. Lucky for us, the world mostly took no notice until we were more fully formed and self-assured. Then, to our collective surprise, the museum world descended on us to study and try out what we had naturally and unselfconsciously invented.

In the late '80s, I commenced on a professional trip through the federal museum landscape of the Smithsonian, where I met sophisticated and intelligent people who worked hard and wanted the best for their museum and the public. But their opinion of what constituted "good" was far different from that of the world I had come from. For the first time I came in contact with fundamental differences in world view. I grew used to, though never comfortable with, the ethical expediencies resorted to by people interested in personal power politics. I learned a lot about strategy, but action was measured in geologic time. The Smithsonian has daring folk who are relatively powerless in moving their museums forward, and less noble folk well equipped to remain entrenched by stifling any action that might prove (to them) destabilizing. While grateful for the experience and the wonderful friends, now family, that I met, I felt I had lost my way.

Then I became a member of the fledgling National Museum of the American Indian, and I came face to face with proud and tenacious Native people who allowed me to understand that they were not kidding when they espoused points of view that were completely foreign to my own. My stay as a member of the senior staff of that museum, under the direction of Rick West, began the part of my museum journey that most changed my intellectual life. I learned that most positions I held—unconsciously or consciously—found counterparts in opposite positions held by my Indian colleagues. Thankfully, they didn't give up on me. And mercifully, one year later, I could intuit their positions without compromising my own. That experience plus extensive travel have taught me that this planet holds countless people who believe things as honorably and fiercely as I do, but often quite differently.

Finally, I went to work for one of the true geniuses of the museum world, Jeshajahu Weinberg, who made it possible for all of his staff to participate in the creation of a masterpiece, the United States Holocaust Memorial Museum. This institution quite fundamentally changed the way museums tell stories, present ideas, and interpret information in an exhibition format. Most important, the museum inspired and provoked reactions from its various publics, from school groups to foreign heads of state, that changed all my notions about visitor behavior and about the potential importance of museums on the world stage.

My career has never had a planned trajectory, but in retrospect I have grown in important ways from every one of these singular experiences.

Given a synthesis of the learning from each of my former "jobs," plus a continued exposure to the truly wonderful and invigorating museums I work with today, I am currently preoccupied museologically with streams of questions—the answers to which might help explain or even forecast the changing roles and definitions of museums that we will encounter in the future. Some of these questions are:

1. What is a civil society, and what roles might museums play in fostering a safer and more humane community? Are museums one of a number of civic pillars that keep society intact?

2. Using a definition of museums as one of our "institutions of memory," what are their emerging organizational affiliations? Perhaps our true family tree is different from the types of organizations we have aligned ourselves with in the past.

3. While collections may have been the underpinning of our work in the past, perhaps that will no longer be the case in the 21st century. What is the appropriate definition of collections in an age with fewer and fewer unique, singular artifacts? Does the creation of exhibitions using tangible three-dimensional environments change our definitions of reproductions, copies, and themed accessories?

4. Should greater importance be accorded to facilities that foster congregant behavior in an age of increasing isolation? If so, is a museum's value as a "meeting place" larger and more fundamental than previously thought? Will museums become (or are they already becoming) a forum for sharing real experiences mediated and enhanced by the presence of many others?

5. How should we integrate the different world views we encounter in our increasingly multicultural society? Can exhibitions present diverse explanations of the same subject matter, while still remaining accurate and understandable to the visitor? If museum artifacts come from societies holding different world views, how might they change our notion of ownership, display, and conservation?

6. When we borrow exhibition and marketing techniques from our entertainment and commercial neighbors, are we compromising or adding to museums' educational birthright?

7. Do management style and corporate culture make museums operate well or poorly, and should our internal style mirror the values of the external society we wish to involve?

The opportunity to draft these few comments has allowed me to understand that there are some unifying threads that run continuously through my career. I still believe, as I said at my educators award ceremony, in the importance of pushing for change. I then quoted Lech Walesa as saying "If you want democracy, make democracy." Since then I have been also guided by Hanan Ashrawi (one of the architects of the Israel-Arab peace accord), who said to me, "If you want peace, make peace." I continue to be committed to action over inaction while trying to use methods that mirror ideals. I remain committed to trial and error and think approximations are the best we can hope for and that they should be reward-ed. I think hand-crafted logical next steps beat ideological dogma. And I remain persuaded of the importance of "and" over the victory of the single answer.

I still believe that museums are important institutions whose collective strength lies partly in their ability to change and be responsive. But I am also mindful that some museums have been and can again be misused for a return to fear-based discrimination and the creation of new justifications for hate. I hope we will all continue on our respective individual journeys to understand, improve, and value them.

My belief is, and has always been, that to be responsible we must include and welcome many different interpretations of museums within our family. Our sense of well-being as members of human society is based equally on a pride in and exploration of our own patrimony and a commitment toward tolerance for others and the importance of the common good. Rational men and women must pre-vail—people who believe in balance, in complexity, and that each of us is entitled to take up equal space, time, and attention.

I am mindful that the old fundamental elements of museums—collec-tions, preservation, contemplation, and excellence—and the methods of presen-tation represented by these values, should not be discarded in our enthusiasm for the new and the next. We must treasure the old and honor the elder while steadi-ly integrating the new to make museums more central and more relevant to a society in which we want to live.

I am more self-conscious about using the word "love" these days, but I still love my work, the people who work in this profession, and the institution called "museum." Further, I still believe that if we love our work and each other, our vis-itor will intuit it. It is not so fashionable to talk of love as it was in the '60s and '70s (and having grown older, seen Holocaust survivors, and lived through the inevitable disappointments and sadness of life, I am more tempered and less naive.) So if asked, as I am occasionally, whether I still believe in the importance of love, I would have to say yes, even if that answer comes out more muted and sub-dued than at the beginning of my working voyage.

CRITICAL ISSUES FOR MUSEUMS IN OUR EXPANDING ROLE

by Alberta Sebolt George

Museums are located in almost every region of our country and attract hundreds of millions of visitors each year. Their collections and programs serve a broad audience, including an ever-growing number of international visitors. These institutions have become an important economic force, as they drive the local, regional, and national economies with collective annual budgets into the billions of dollars.

Museums nevertheless struggle with external issues of public perception as well as internal issues of vision-building and developing consensus among staff on institutional priorities. Defining a vision that makes sense and remains in balance with the pressing need for financial stability isn't easy, but it is critical if we are to achieve our mission within the public dimension.

Museums are unique institutions that preserve our nation's culture; through their commitment to research and education, they share remarkable collections and knowledge with the world. Our communities would be very different without the experiences provided by museums, and we must open our doors wider to enlighten and enrich the lives of millions of student and adult learners. These efforts will, I am sure, magnify the results today and ensure vitality tomorrow.

As with all successful endeavors, to achieve their goals museums must be attentive to performance, productivity, and sound business management. We must be able to balance a sense of urgency with the need for accuracy and timely delivery. As a nation we are experiencing an era of intense global competition and a reshaping of our culture. Mindful that our economic progress in the last few years has been significant, we continue to be concerned about productivity and our ability to compete.

The need to align the growth potential of the United States with the improvement of our national educational system positions the focus on our public schools. In the education of a nation, however, as with that of an individual, the greater part of learning occurs outside of the school or formal setting. We learn what we live. While the classroom offers a special kind of learning, our communities and the rich resources of museums have an important role to play. To educate for life—not merely for living—is the real mandate; it has become obvious that museums can contribute enormously to personal development. Everything we see and hear contributes to what we know and who we are.

There are new paradigms afloat, and just as old global economic patterns are giving way to new ones, so will old practices that once seemed appropriate for museums. We have always placed education at the forefront of maintaining a democracy, but as we have become more anxious about the future the focus on education has intensified. The opportunity is before us to help direct the winds of change.

We cannot, however, achieve and maintain the desired level of programming without addressing all the issues facing our institutions. We need to transform our organizations if we are to achieve our goals of service in the public dimension. Reform includes making choices and often "raising the bar" for our performance. There are competing mandates for our finite resources, and we must be clear about all the issues that arise within our operation. These are formidable times for all organizations, but the stretch for museums is perhaps the greatest.

To make those tough decisions, we must know who we truly are and initiate whatever changes are necessary to keep museums relevant. As resources become more scarce, we must ensure that our work is seen as important within the world. A mission firmly placed on the high ground does not shelter us from the changing fabric of the world around us. Those same social, economic, and political trends shaping society today will influence the future of museums.

Nonprofit institutions simply do not have the reserves to protect us from the vicissitudes of the economy or the shifting demands and constraints of the community. This often means we must plan better and run faster than the pack, just to stay in the race.

Also crucial to our success will be museum leaders who can look outward, engaging the community to achieve a new level of public involvement, while nurturing critical thinking and rigorous scholarship. Leaders must not only manage change, but must get ahead of the change process. Leadership involves bringing a management team to a point where it can develop solutions that may even require a stunning transformation. It means taking risks and making moves even when we don't have the answer.

More than ever before, our performance is dependent upon a well-functioning team that understands our mission and mandate and is responsible for getting results. Although there are always differing perspectives, embracing individual differences will always enhance the product. If strong educational programs are to be the collective goal, then all corners of the institution must buy into the priority. Building consensus is not easy, but it is worth the diligence and perseverance it takes. For staff to have a valid sense of their stake in the future, they must develop a valid image of that future; without a well-defined image it is difficult to address the critical issues. Developing that image allows us to put strategies in place to achieve commitment and empower the team.

Although we are passionate about our educational goals, the public and private financial support for these initiatives has not grown over the last quarter century, in spite of the expansion of our audience's expectations. Just as in the public sector, the cost of education is dear and not always perceived by the users. For most cultural organizations the true cost of the program/concert is twice the fee charged the attendee. Without increased support the cost of programs is often prohibitive and will work against broadening the audience. The future will depend upon some thoughtful planning to stabilize the financial underpinnings of these public service initiatives.

Over the course of the last decade, every level of government has been pressed to deal with the delivery of more services with fewer resources. We are not likely to find increased support from that sector. Today, in addition, nonprofits are subject to a kind of scrutiny that endangers our very existence. Attempts to tax nonprofits are increasing and work against our efforts to deliver public service. Often emerging from the public's misconceptions that museums are wealthy (after all, look at those collections!), these misguided actions reflect a dangerous error in public perception. Clearly, we need to establish our worth or risk becoming irrelevant. Fulfilling our real mission as educational institutions helps assure us a place in our nation's educational and cultural present and future.

Critical issues in this decade are different from those we faced a quarter century ago when I first became involved with museums. At that time, the debate focused on the place and worth of an institution's educational functions. Often heard were these questions: Did we really need education departments? After all, weren't the people we wanted in our institutions educated and ready to comprehend our work? Did we really need to develop strategies to bridge the gap between visitor and environment? It was an internal debate that created tensions between functions and would ultimately force important changes in our focus and our goals.

Today, on the other hand, the debate is more externally focused—on market forces, searching for audience growth, coming to grips with the competition for leisure time, and analyzing the demographics of our audience. The trends provoke us to evaluate and justify our work within the realities of a new world environment.

From our vantage point in the last days of the last decade of the 20th century, it may be difficult to remember just how pioneering museums have been—or just how far they have come—in the pursuit of public service. Our standards of delivery and of excellence have changed, as have the expectations of our audience. Once upon a time, in my lifetime, education in museums was defined by the thoughtful presentation of exhibits based on solid scholarship. Perhaps a program or two for students might run in an adjacent gallery or sub-level classroom, bringing aspects of the exhibit to the level of young learners.

When we are at our best today, that experience occurs as an integral part of planning an exhibit as a simultaneous event, tour, program, or studio. The process of program and exhibit planning has expanded in concept to include not only the scholarship derived from the research but concern for the visitor's experience and point of orientation. Seeking information about the motivations of learners, different patterns of learning, and visitor behavior, we have learned a great deal along the way—including perhaps, how to listen differently. In our pursuit of excellence, we've asked more questions, received candid feedback, and developed a growing awareness of our audience.

As we look to the future, we now know that meaningful experiences have the power needed to bridge the gap between the museum as environment and the visitor as learner and will, I am certain, advance our mission more than any other initiative. Researching and understanding the process of learning are essential, but unless we apply that knowledge to everything we do—the exhibit plans, the labels, the teaching strategies, and all our communication—we will not be successful in expanding and diversifying our audience. Our success will be measured by the experiences we can provoke for our visitors. With renewed attention to the reform of our nation's educational system, we have a chance to share in the process. Given our awesome and uncommon resources, we have an exciting opportunity to become effective partners in addressing this national priority.

We've had good results in creating powerful coalitions over the last two decades, and that track record serves us well. Our work with schools succeeds when teachers and museum staff develop a shared assessment of needs, an understanding of each other's skills and objectives, and sufficient levels of trust and communication. We have an important role to play as we grow tomorrow's stakeholders in today's museums. We must foster openness and awareness, and nurture conceptual thinking through engagement opportunities and open new doors of understanding for our nation's youth and tomorrow's museum visitor.

It can be done, and I share an example from the world I know best. Today, the Old Sturbridge Village is a re-created rural 19th-century New England town on a landscape of more than 200 acres. Serving as a major cultural attraction, it welcomes almost a half-million visitors each year: 350,000 national and international tourists as a part of the cultural tourism market and more than 100,000 teachers, scholars, youth groups, and student and adult learners. Regionally, Old Sturbridge Village strengthens the quality of life in the Northeast. As a cultural amenity, we not only contribute to the economy and give character to our community, but also make the region a more pleasing place to live.

But it is through the experiences we create for our visitors that our public dimension is served and image will grow. Yes, we perform the many functions of museums as stewards of our heritage, and our collection is central to our mission. Because of the nature of this collection, however, and its focus on history, we've needed to focus strategies on overcoming our culture's sharp distinction between past and present to create meaningful experiences. Thinking of the Village community as a stage has helped enormously, providing a setting and easily placing learning within a context. Each strategy creates or amplifies the museum as a place where visitors develop a sense of the past and sometimes even imagine themselves in a different time. A priority for us is to enhance the visitor's capacity to be historically informed while at the same time providing an opportunity to escape and simply have fun. Programs provide focus and orientation, engage the imagination, increase knowledge, and still give pleasure. Sometimes they even allow the visitor to see the world differently.

Museums can assume an important position within the world of teaching and learning. They have, in many instances, established themselves as legitimate and effective laboratories for field-based learning. As they embrace their role within public education, they also position themselves to be a more significant part of the lives of more people for generations to come.

The pace of change has accelerated over the past decade, and futurists tell us we will not see it relax during the foreseeable future. We must keep listening and learning as we anticipate more challenges and further destabilization. Things may settle down as time goes by, but they'll settle differently. Our world will never be the same again, and the odds are that neither will museums.

STAYING WITH THE BIG PICTURE

by Danielle Rice

Upon receiving the AAM Education Committee award in 1988, I made the following points in my acceptance speech: (1) Museums are in a perfect position to work towards improving society because they represent the best examples of human creative endeavor and because visitors come to museums predisposed to be inspired and moved. (2) Museum educators can make a significant difference in people's lives if they remember to work from the assumption that all people are basically good, intelligent, and creative; if they keep the focus on people as opposed to objects; and if they strive to treat everyone, including themselves, with complete respect. This last piece was in admonition against the then-prevailing sentiment that museum educators were "underdogs" within the museum hierarchy. Almost 10 years later, it is useful to reflect on these recommendations and to consider the issues facing the field today.

One of the major challenges that has confronted my institution in the past decade has been the chronic shortage of funds and the need, in this market economy, to become more savvy about earned income. In some ways, this pressure has also made my museum more audience oriented, playing right into many of my museum education objectives. We have improved the interpretation of the permanent collections, expanded our programs for families, and experimented with new technologies as a way of reaching new audiences. On the whole, the museum has become more visitor friendly and accessible. We have also initiated an interdepartmental diversity committee that has helped the institution prioritize diversity issues and work towards bringing more people of color through our galleries.

At the same time, however, admission rates have doubled, the museum store has grown and expanded into several pockets of space throughout the building, the restaurant and cafeteria have become more upscale, and the pressure to make money from tour groups and space rentals has intensified. The shortage of space and staff resources pits educational programs against income-generating ones. To make itself more appealing, the museum has also had to become more entertaining, providing a festive atmosphere at the popular Wednesday evening programs, and positioning itself to compete for audiences looking for a classy place to hold a party. At least one major exhibition has had to be canceled for lack of corporate sponsorship, and while cancelation of shows is fairly rare, exhibition-related educational programming is often held hostage to funding shortages.

When we succumb to the pressure to justify museum activity in economic terms, we inadvertently begin thinking about our audiences as customers instead of citizens. Jim Wood, director of the Art Institute of Chicago, once noted that economic authority of an institution that serves customers derives from the assumption that the customer is always right. For museums, this would imply that current sales and attendance figures would provide the final measure of success and that programs or exhibitions that cannot deliver the figures would therefore have to be curtailed. On the other hand, the authority of an institution dedicated to providing educational and inspirational opportunities for citizens derives from a societal consensus that this experience is essential and enduring and deserves to be made a priority. If the public is treated as consumer, the museum will target very different audiences than if the public is seen as citizens equally deserving of opportunity.

But does a consensus currently exist that museums are socially worthwhile educational institutions? In today's climate, this is not always easy to gauge. I am referring in particular to the general anti-expert, anti-intellectual tenor of today's media and popular culture. That a tension exists at present between the interests of the viewing public and those of the professional world of artists, scholars, collectors, and critics who define and legitimize the work of the museum is clear from the number of museum-related controversies that have erupted over the past 10 years. Insofar as art museums are concerned, the tension results from conflicting assumptions about art's social role. Regardless of personal political beliefs, most visitors assume that museums define art in absolute terms and expect institutions to act accordingly by showing art that is readily accessible and matches their own definition of "good" and "worthwhile" art. Similarly, art world insiders and museum professionals, while they cannot be said to share identical views, are nevertheless united by a liberal relativism when it comes to definitions of art and a strong adherence to notions that art and scholarship should challenge established beliefs and views. Thus, in this respect, the views of museum publics and museum professionals can be said to be almost mutually exclusive. While museum professionals everywhere struggle with the need to appeal to ever-increasing audiences, those very audiences, aided by a media that is eager to label museums as elitist or representing fringe interests, are finding the experts to be patronizing or seemingly opposed to maintaining cultural traditions and values.

Partly as a result of these tensions and also because of developments in the various disciplines that inform museum work, the role of museum educators has shifted. Over the past 10 years, museum educators have come to view themselves more as cultural brokers, mediating between the different cultures of museum scholars and museum audiences. The new weight given to visitors' experiences and ways of knowing in the museum has resulted in this revision of the museum's educative function and, subsequently, the role of the museum educator. New information derived from planned evaluation, surveys, and focus groups about the nature of the visitor experience has resulted in a new attitude of respect for and interest in the perspectives of so-called novice viewers. But we have also begun to realize how little we actually know about what and how visitors learn in our galleries and what impact museum educators have when participating in formal education through school tours, curriculum development, and teacher training. The recent debates about the role of a constructivist theories of learning and their role in museum education illustrate this shortcoming.

Constructivism is a term broadly applied to a cluster of theories stating that learners construct their own knowledge. In other words, people think and create their own understanding about things, building on their own internal constructions of reality. The fundamental principles, as they have come to be applied to education, derive primarily from the discipline of cognitive psychology and in particular the work of American educational philosopher John Dewey, Swiss psychologist Jean Piaget, Russian psychologist Lev Vygotsky, and their many followers.[1] In the past 20 years, the work of educational psychologists Jerome Bruner and Howard Gardner has also been very influential. The constructivist approach in education is consistent with the postmodernist de-privileging of any one narrative to explain the history of art. These theories, combined with the self-criticism that seems to be endemic to the museum profession, have convinced some educators to pull back completely from their function as transmitters of information. After all, if one concludes that visitors' ways of deriving meaning from art are equal to those of museum professionals, then there is no particular necessity to introduce visitors to the values or ideas of the experts.

Furthermore, in our insecurity about the legitimacy of the museum education endeavor, we rush to jump on the latest theoretical bandwagon before fully understanding its implications. While constructivism does indeed seem to be a useful cluster of theories with broad applicability to museum education, there are other theories to be explored as well. Ideas coming out of anthropology and rhetoric, for example, have invigorated educational theory with a neo-pragmatist approach that sees learners as belonging to particular cultures or discourse communities. In this theoretical framework, educators, instead of considering how people construct knowledge, have to be concerned with issues of task: specifically, questions such as what do we want to accomplish with this specific audience at this specific moment. Because museums are being used more and more as recreational, leisure-time, social environments, not all people visit to learn. Thus, in some situations, the task of museum educators may be to encourage people who have come with a different agenda to become learners.

The weight of having to legitimate the actions of a large, expensive, complex institution with an inspiring educational mission can make museum professionals forget that most people come to the museum for recreation and pleasure. Patently absurd is the fear, often expressed in professional meetings and journals, that if museums pander too much to visitor tastes they will sell out and become like Disney World. Museum visitors know the difference just as they know the difference between a cheeseburger and a filet mignon, but like most of us in this culture, they happily consume both. Disney's menu is very limited, offering visitors only a restricted brand of pleasure through consumerism. Museums have many more treats in store: pleasure through enlightenment, pleasure through awareness, pleasure through contact with real objects (so desirable in today's culture of simulation), pleasure through enriched contact with oneself and others, pleasure through association with glamour. These are all legitimate delights that visitors seek and that museums can offer.

In the past, we've defined these differences as those between entertainment and education. But these definitions are misleading because people loved to be entertained by learning. A more useful distinction might be between a passive utilitarian model of pleasure, achieved as at Disney World primarily through sensory stimulation and the opportunity to purchase souvenirs, and an expressivist model of pleasure, achieved as in museums through self-growth and social contact.

Finally, museums should work to distinguish themselves from consumer-oriented entertainment extravaganzas like Disney World or calculating, multimedia marketing enterprises like Niketown by taking a public and moral stance on major social issues affecting quality of life. I still believe, as I did 10 and even 20 years ago, that museums function symbolically as well as practically. As symbols, museums embody what a culture values most and preserve what it considers most meaningful. They are icons of enlightenment and the human aspiration for truth and beauty. Because of this important symbolic function, it is essential for museums to take carefully considered ethical positions on the shortcomings of today's society. Museums should embrace their symbolic role as leaders of the fight to improve our world.

While straining to survive and flourish, we should make large and visible gestures in defending this symbolic, ethical role. It isn't enough to provide a small percentage (on the average, museums only reach about 20 percent of all people) with interesting and thought-provoking exhibitions and programs. We need to play a leadership role on a large scale. For example, I am one of a number of staff at the Philadelphia Museum of Art urging the institution to eliminate its admissions fees. To me, this represents a moral imperative. Such a policy would underline our mission of broad accessibility to all people. We would also contradict, consciously and intentionally, the current greed-oriented ethos of our culture. As a large institution dedicated to quality, we could indicate that we believe and support the notion that the best things in life should be free, thereby modeling by example the understanding that the profit motive is not in the interest of the greater good.

At a recent long-range planning retreat, I was involved in a discussion on audience development. Our committee, composed of museum staff and trustees, kept returning to the fact that the museum is competing with a number of other institutions for the attention of a finite group of people with diminishing amounts of leisure time. The discussion focused on how we could make ourselves more desirable and therefore more competitive. During the debate, my mind wandered to my own hectic, pressured life as a working professional and parent: how little time I actually have to spend with my children, how hard it is to make the decision to go to a museum. I remembered how at a certain moment in my youth in the 1970s it actually looked as though people in the future would have more, rather than less, leisure time, and the work week would get shorter. At that moment, I startled myself and my group by blurting out: "What if instead of competing for the same audiences, museums were to take a vastly different position that would really change the way society functioned? What if museums were to become advocates of a four-day work week? Consider what would happen to museums and cultural institutions if people actually had an extra day off every week." An embarrassed silence followed. One of the trustees on the committee broke the tension by joking, "I'm not sure what that would do to the museum's corporate support."

We moved on, but the possibility of a vastly different vision of the world lingered. Working to improve society is what museum work has always represented for me and for so many of my colleagues. Given the pressures and challenges of museum work, we sometimes lose track of that idealistic objective. But we need both vision and practical skills. Continuing to improve the day-to-day functioning of the institutions we work in while taking and holding visionary positions will enable us not only to engage in the debate about how museums can function as agents of social change but also to broaden the parameters of that debate.

In my 1988 acceptance speech I said: "The first step is to keep the big scheme in mind at all times." I still believe that. It is much easier to struggle with the practical realities of too little time, too little money, too little staff, if we keep the big picture in mind. If anything has changed for me over the years, it is perhaps that the picture has gotten even bigger than I had previously thought was possible.

REFERENCES

1. For a review of constructivism, see "Educational Theory" in *Museums: Places of Learning* by G. E. Hein and M. Alexander (Washington, D.C.: American Association of Museums, 1998), pp. 29-39; and "The Good, the Bad, and the Ugly: The Many Faces of Constructivism" in *Educational Researcher* 24, no. 7: 5-12.

SOME THOUGHTS ON
IMPROVING EDUCATION IN MUSEUMS

by Judith White

To make museums effective educational institutions, professionals working today must address two critical issues. One is the effort to broaden the base of institutions truly committed to education. The second is the need to maintain a high standard of creativity in developing educational programs, exhibits, and research.

ISSUE ONE: COMMITMENT TO EDUCATION

Institutional commitment to education—or, more important, the lack of thereof—is an issue that has been with us for years. The authors of *Museums for a New Century* commented on this problem, suggesting that there was a lack of consensus about what learning in museums is. They gave two reasons for that situation: the absence of a "philosophical framework"[1] for museum learning theory and a conflict of values within museums. They described this as "a tension of values that is inherent in the very mission of museums. Stated quite simply, the concerns of preservation, and the demands of public access are a contradiction lived out in every institution."[2]

Looking around museums today, I see that not much has changed. By and large, what the *Museums'* authors described in 1984 is still true. A majority of museums list education among a number of conflicting goals. (A few museums simply pay lip service to it.) These mixed priorities are reflected in what the museums do (or do not do) in terms of education: low budgets, confused exhibitions, and lackluster public programs.

Making a museum an effective educational institution is not an easy task. It requires commitment throughout—from curators, conservators, exhibit designers, and educators. You cannot delegate the job of education to museum educators or another subgroup within the museum. Doing that is like asking the tail to wag the dog. For the tail to wag, you need the body of the dog to work. That body is the whole institution. Without its support, museum professionals working to improve education will be waging an uphill battle.

There are, of course, a number of museums that clearly stand out as effective educational institutions. Why are they successful? It's pretty clear. All have one thing in common: a shared philosophical framework for museum learning and an institutional commitment to promote that kind of experience. In these museums the whole body is working for education.

According to *Museums for a New Century*, there is interest in better understanding learning in museums. As the *Museums'* authors state, "There is interest among educators and administrators alike in formulating museum learning theory more clearly."[3] The exemplary museums have begun to formulate such a theory. Why aren't they more widely imitated? Why have their ideas not been more broadly adopted by other institutions?

I suspect that museum staff have other things on their minds besides learning. And there is competition for priorities. The authors of *Museums* observed that there is "a tension of values that is inherent in the very mission of museums . . . the concerns of preservation and the demands of public access are a contradiction lived out in every institution."[4] Today, it is clear that a "tension of values" within museums still exists. But something new has been added. The conflict is no longer simply between the "concerns of preservation" and the "demands of public access." Today many museums have learned that there is profit to be had in public programs and exhibition. New players have entered the fray: marketing and fund raising. So conflict now occurs even within the arena of public access itself.

Eleanor Heartney alludes to this conflict in an article in the *Washington Post*. She comments on new trends in public exhibition that she feels threaten to compromise the veracity of museum interpretation. "These new trends are driven in part by a public that wants more for its leisure-time dollar . . . prodded by ever higher museum admission charges. . . . These desires feed museum exhibition policies. Government cutbacks and the increased competition for private and corporate funding have forced institutions to rely heavily on ticket and gift shop sales."[5]

How will the quality of the museum educational experience fare in this new marketing climate? It could improve, or it could go under. It all depends on where the institution's commitment to education lies. Is it in the body of the dog, or only in the tail?

ISSUE TWO: CREATIVITY AND INNOVATION

Those of us working in the educational arena need to make sure that we are as creative as possible in the coming years. This task is not nearly so difficult as getting institutions to commit to education, because creativity is an internal task that most of us can do something about. Why do I raise this issue? In part because I think that we in education, exhibition, and visitor studies could profit from a bit of stirring up.

Over the past 20 or so years there has been a marked increase in our professionalism. There are now established meetings, committees, journals, and degrees offered in museology and education. While I think this is overall a positive step for museums, I would like to speak a word of caution. The dark side of professionalism is the tendency to institutionalize practices—including ways of working and thinking. Of course, establishing work practices is not necessarily bad. (And for certain museum professions, such as conservation, it is a necessity.) But those of us who create exhibits, programs, and other means of communicating with the public need to be constantly inventing and reinventing. And perhaps we need to be reinventing ourselves.

I was appalled recently when a friend told me that the school programs in her museum were developed 10 years ago. Then I thought back to some places where I have worked. I am sure that programs I invented are still going on.

I am wary of museum professionals becoming too complacent and/or not thinking for themselves. Why does your new science center have to look like dozens of others? Does your museum have to have docent tours? Why build another tropical rain forest in your zoo? I am concerned that students in museum education are being trained by people who themselves are products of schools of education. I am fearful that courses may become standardized. Are we still teaching with the same old stories?

I suggest that those of us working to develop programs and exhibits are probably at our most productive if we can maintain a level of naiveté, looking at each situation as if for the first time. We might follow the advice of a designer friend of mine. He says each time he designs an exhibit, it is a completely new experience.

So, do I have any advice for what museum professionals should do about these issues? Mostly, I would suggest that you think about them and try to figure out ways to address them in terms of the job that you are doing at the time or the jobs you might be seeking. Besides that I offer a few suggestions.

REGARDING EDUCATIONAL COMMITMENT

If you are just entering the museum profession, I suggest that you seek out institutions that appear to have a commitment to education. Those are places where you can grow personally. And you may be able to pioneer new ideas for exhibits and programs.

For those of you who have been in museums for a bit longer, I suggest that you work toward getting out of the tail of the dog. Put yourselves in positions where you can influence the institutional priorities of a particular museum, or of museums in general. That might mean becoming a director of a museum of manageable size and helping to guide its direction. That's what Michael Spock and Alan Friedman did at the Children's Museum in Boston and the New York Hall of Science. Or, you may have to do what Frank Oppenheimer did: He started his own museum—the Exploratorium.

REGARDING CREATIVITY

If you are new to the field, I suggest that you question museum practices—constantly. Go out and see what is happening for yourself. Watch visitors. Read widely.

If you are a veteran in museums, I suggest that you take time out. Find a way to look at your job from a different vantage point. Do some programmatic sorting every now and then. Recently, I packed up 20 years of household objects. I had to make choices about which possessions were important enough to haul 2,000 miles in a van. In the process I discovered many objects that no longer "worked" for me because they belonged to a time past. Look at your museum in a similar way. Can you streamline your programs and open up new avenues for innovation?

If you are an evaluator, or write grants to hire evaluators and researchers, I suggest that you find ways to increase the depth of visitor studies. We still know very little about how people learn in museums. Try to ask some larger questions about the nature of the museum experience. Today we have many more people doing visitor studies than ever before. But most of these studies are of the nuts-and-bolts variety. They can improve an individual exhibit. But they are not really about the nature of informal learning or how people can learn in a museum. We need more studies that push the envelope, that create controversy, and raise issues. We need more studies that will engage a museum's entire staff in discussion of the museum learning experience.

Whom am I learning from today? Where are the future directions and sources of my ideas? I find these questions difficult to answer. Perhaps that is because I tend to get ideas from many different places. My mind behaves rather like a hunter-gatherer. It scans the environment and selects interesting bits. Who knows where the next one may turn up? It may be in a museum, in a hardware store, or at the dentist's office. Some tidbits apply immediately to work that I am doing; others are stored away for future use. However, I do find that when I am doing a project, I come across an amazing number of bits all over the place. Perhaps it is because my mind is tuned in to the subject and selectively spots things like ripe berries on a bush.

I am also an omnivorous reader. It is a diet that sustains my personal curiosity and also comes in handy when I work. I enjoy dealing with disparate phenomena and am delighted when I discover similarities among them.

There is not a specific "whom" that I am learning from. There are a variety of sources. I am quite taken by Michael Spock's video studies of museum experiences. They have raised new questions in my mind about the museum experience. And I am intrigued by the art/science creations of artist/designer Ned Kahn. They have shown me the value of open-ended exhibits and a sensory-based approach to learning.

I currently admire the writing style of Timothy Ferris, author of *The Whole Shebang: A State-of-the-Universe(s) Report*. He has an ability to explain difficult concepts in a clear and friendly manner. I also admire the lighthearted, no-nonsense approach of many of the Klutz Press books. All these authors have helped make science a more approachable subject for many. That is what science museums should do.

I find inspiration in numerous people that I read about. Two I have been thinking about recently are Cézanne and Giacometti. Both struggled for a lifetime to understand how to wrestle a three-dimensional object onto a two-dimensional format. Imagine applying similar persistence to understanding museum learning.

Is there a set of books that I depend on for museum work? As I was writing this, I went to my bookshelves to see which books I have looked at repeatedly. I have some favorites in education and museum practices, but I realized that I have not looked at them for some time. They were very useful once, but not so much now. The books that seem to stand the test of time are children's books: Mother Goose, classic fairy tales, and authors such as Beatrix Potter, Dr. Seuss, E. B. White, A. A. Milne. I come back to these books every now and then to get ideas flowing. Perhaps, that is because their stories are universal ones that give insight into basic human thoughts and feelings.

Where the future directions and sources of my learning will be, I cannot predict. They may be inspired by projects that I am doing. Or maybe I will come across them in a museum, dentist's office, or hardware store. Who knows? I would prefer to follow the example of Stuart Little:

> Stuart rose from the ditch, climbed into his car, and started up the road that led toward the north. The sun was just coming up over the hills on his right. As he peered ahead into the great land that stretched before him, the way seemed long. But the sky was bright, and he somehow felt he was headed in the right direction.[6]

REFERENCES

1. Ellen Cochran Hicks, ed., *Museums for a New Century: A Report of the Commission on Museums for a New Century* (Washington, D.C.: American Association of Museums, 1984), p. 57.

2. Ibid., pp. 57-58.

3. Ibid., p. 57.

4. Ibid., p. 58.

5. Eleanor Heartney, "Now Playing at a Museum Near You," *Washington Post*, Sept. 8, 1997, p. 23.

6. E. B. White, *Stuart Little* (New York: Harper & Brothers, 1945), p. 131.

CRITICAL ISSUES FOR MAKING ART MUSEUMS EFFECTIVE EDUCATIONAL INSTITUTIONS

by Patterson B. Williams

Over the years, I've increasingly come to believe that one's point of view usually determines estimates of the value and meaningfulness of almost everything—including the artwork that museums collect. Yet I still also believe in the traditional role of curatorial experts to make judgments about what art museums collect and display. In a similar vein, I believe that in my own relativistic personal world, where right and wrong are not based on universal truths, I must make choices and try to do more good than bad.

I begin this article about museum accessibility and education with a discussion of the curator's role because it is a pivotal factor affecting the critical issues facing art museums. I also believe that all museums in the United States are essentially public institutions no matter where they get their annual operating money. When I use the word "public," I don't mean "government" but that museums have responsibilities to the broadest possible spectrum of people in their communities.

Not everyone would agree with these two premises about art museum collections—that experts should choose them and that museums should make them accessible to very broad publics. In fact, if these two contrary factors are the basis of determining an art museum's priorities, life inside the museum will always be a matter of starts, stops, and hesitations, of going backward and forward at the same time.

There are many days when I wish it were easier to determine priorities in my museum. But when I daydream about alternatives, I don't like what I see. For instance, if we were willing to let the broad public choose the art we display, we might have many contrasting galleries of art, each designed to please a different constituency. The best paid and most powerful people on staff would act primarily as facilitators of community-based decisions about art. These new staff members would have some knowledge of art, but they would also be experts in getting groups of citizens to come to consensus and would probably specialize in communication with a single culture group. But I don't like the idea of bowing primarily to the differences among us in the public sphere or of abandoning the advantages of subtle discriminations and in-depth knowledge as the primary basis of decision making about collecting art.

On the other hand, I am also uncomfortable with the vision of a museum that is guided by unquestioned expertise. Such an institution reaches only those who either agree with the experts or who are willing to consciously or unconsciously cede judgment about what is valuable and meaningful in art rather than consider the art themselves. In this kind of museum, true aesthetic enjoyment involving personal values is not going to be the norm.

Today's art museums face four critical issues that have enormous impact on their ability to make their collections accessible to broad audiences. They are :

■ bringing together curators and educators to create museum leadership focused on making artworks accessible

■ finding effective ways to respond pragmatically to our public support base and to our private support base

■ providing the public with the most intelligent, insightful, and well-articulated cases for the meaningfulness and enjoyment of the objects in our galleries

■ providing educational/access services to individual visitors

CURATORS AND EDUCATORS

We severely limit our public service goals when we harbor a petty and destructive kind of discord between these two groups of staff. There are such interesting and important issues and ideas that should be discussed in "mixed company" of curators and educators. And for all kinds of strange and silly reasons, we seldom take up these issues except as separate groups.

For example, I'm currently trying to understand and sort out the relationship between the practice of connoisseurship and the development of an understanding of how artworks come into being ("context" for short). This issue has been on my mind since I served as project director for an exhibition of Egyptian art. Before we started work on the show, the objects were selected and the catalogue researched and written by curators and university Egyptologists. A combination of a high level of connoisseurship and scholarship resulted in a good selection of objects and a useful compilation of current and past research related to the objects. My job, along with other staff, was to come up with an installation that would help visitors have personally meaningful experiences with these objects. Should I concentrate on the archaeological discovery of the objects, their aesthetic qualities, or the miracle of how they came into being? I decided that concentrating on context would be the best way to both respect the objects and draw families and adult visitors to them. But I kept thinking of connoisseurship and context as opposing tracks. Did it make sense for connoisseurship to be the primary principle for selecting objects and context to be the principal means for finding meaningful experiences with those same objects? I've discussed this question with colleagues in the education department, my director and deputy director (both former curators), our docents, some trustees, members of the public in the show, and even with my husband (several times) and our next door neighbors. Now I need to go and talk to the curators with whom I collaborate. I'm sure I'll go that far but I think I should go farther. But will I?

I've already developed some passionate views on this question. I've been driven for years, even decades, by questions about these two big ruling (dueling?) principles that guide so much of the intellectual and emotional life in American art museums. I'm ready now with a principle of my own: Art museums should select the art they display primarily by the rule of connoisseurship. And then, the minute the artwork has been selected, they should switch gears and explore and celebrate the creation of the marvelous objects they collect and preserve. The mainstream art museum of the 20th century has celebrated mainly the selecting of objects. I keep asking people "Once the artwork is selected, isn't the most wonderful and important thing about it the miracle of how it came into existence?"

This is, for me, a big idea, and I'd like to understand more about connoisseurship as I continue to think about it. Maybe I'm imagining more conflict than there would be. Maybe I'm just looking for the easy way and don't want any challenges. Or maybe this is a critically important issue to discuss over a long period in an open dialogue. There are issues here that can lead to creating a better museum for the public and to sharpening our ability to work together and capturing the best of what context and connoisseurship have to offer. Certainly curators and educators should have a forum for discussing such ideas, but in my experience this seldom occurs in art museums. How many of my colleagues have such a forum? Do we buttonhole each other in the hallway on the way to the ladies/men's rooms? Do we talk about it for five minutes at the end of a meeting about next year's exhibition schedule? How can art museum educators, curators, and managers create good, substantive conversation among curators and educators? Some would say this can only happen in small groups and with people who know each other well and have a level of trust. If so, how can a museum restructure itself so that this happens?

Here are some suggestions (from an educator's point of view) for stopping the nonsense that prevents educators and curators from talking about the issues they share. Encourage educators to become more assertive. Encourage curators to willingly share power with educators. And demand that educators and curators deal honestly and courteously with their differences and continue to be different in their day-to-day tasks, expertise, and values. Ever since I read Neil Harris's analysis of the differences between curators and educators, I've become more convinced that they should lead museums together. Here is Harris's description:

It might be argued that American museums today contain two cultures, difficult to define but quite distinctive. The one is committed to its cache of objects, their protection, identification, and categorization, suspicious of deviation from scholarly disciplines, humanistic in rhetoric, analytic in method, apolitical or marginally conservative, institutionally traditionalist if intellectually innovative. The other is absorbed by the corps of visitors, their study, instruction, and nurture, eager for institutional experiment, positivistic in method if humanistic in aim, politically more activist, socially critical, progressive and ameliorist by temperament. Often, but not always, the two cultures divide into curatorial-educational ranks. But there are in each group deviants, subversive[s], or liberators, according to one's viewpoint, complicating any effort at analysis. The divisions are contestants for budgetary support, staff positions, trustee interest, and policy making. Their confrontation not only makes the museum director's life interesting; at many institutions it is the tension that brings life and energy to the larger whole. These are different visions of purpose and meaning, forcing choices continually to be made.

(from the keynote address at the American Association of Art Museum Directors conference, June 1989.)

Educators and curators, with their wonderful differences in values, temperament, and even the kinds of intelligence they bring to the table, should work hand in hand and on an absolutely equal footing to make collections more accessible to a broader public.

Here are some suggestions for educators: Become more expert about your collections, learn to deal as effectively and assertively as you can with human conflict, and get a therapist to help you.

Here are some suggestions for curators: Look to a new future rather than to the past, and stop worrying about what you might lose if you share power with people who are not like you in some ways. Articulate and share the reasons for the decisions you make about what you collect thoroughly and honestly. And get a therapist to help you.

My call for therapy for educators and curators is made somewhat seriously. Many of the problems of curators and educators stem from insecurities, jealousies, and hurt feelings. Managers can make a difference, but personal change for curators and educators is also needed.

PUBLIC AND PRIVATE SUPPORT

Museums find it much easier to respond productively to their responsibilities for private sources of funding than for public funding. When I watch this happen over and over again, I'm struck by the simple fact that private funding comes with a real human being. The funder has a personality—whether charming or challenging, demanding or compliant—and some kind of passion for art. We should understand and respect the private donor's feelings and interests and act on them. We should nurture these donors to increase both their passion for making their collections publicly accessible and their understanding of the subtleties of collecting. We should encourage private donors to proudly fund the long-term accessibility needs of their collections, including conservation, storage, installation, and education projects.

On the other hand, public funds, often in very large amounts (directly and indirectly), come to us from Mr. and Mrs. Nobody. There is a lot of rhetoric about the responsibility that these funds demand, but most of it is so vague as to be impossible to really act upon. The museum family must make these responsibilities integral to the daily work of the institution. This is no small challenge. What on earth do we do with mission statements that say we will be accessible to all citizens? It is a hard question to answer, unless we decide that merely being open to the public represents a successful fulfillment of this mission. On the other hand, when government officials act as arbiters of our success or failure, they usually have too little interest and time to understand the complexity of museum issues. Curators, educators, and all other museum staff with critical roles in caring for and presenting collections should work hard together to articulate honest and concrete institutional values and effective programs that fulfill whatever aspects of this public responsibility they choose to take to heart.

ENJOYMENT AND MEANINGFULNESS

Many years ago in a lecture at the Denver Art Museum, Mortimer Adler gently berated museums and art experts for not being willing to say why they believed an artwork to be excellent. As an educator who would like to be helpful to the public and loyal to curatorial expertise, this is something I long for. It requires a willingness to articulate such opinions—to recall first seeing an object; to look again and again at the object in comparison to others; and, most difficult of all, to eloquently articulate this process and the subtle qualities of the object as well as the subtle states of mind that comprise a judgment of excellence. Certainly, there would be some corresponding discussion from members of the public about any such decisions we decided to articulate in this way. Museums that take this approach would not be arbiters of taste in the sense of dictating what visitors should value, but they would be in a powerful position as institutions that act thoughtfully and with discrimination about complex choices. They would have the confidence and respect to share the details of these decisions with their visitors.

INDEPENDENT VISITORS

For about eight years, the education department in which I work has acted on the belief that the most important way to enhance public experience in museums is to focus primarily on adult and family visitors who are on their own in the museum galleries. This has caused us to restructure education staff and assign collections to educators just as we do to curators. It also led to creating pairs of curators and educators as critical units for decisions about gallery installations and to promoting these educators, called "master teachers," to positions equal to those of the curators with whom they work.

School programs may not be the most important focus for museum education, and training programs for volunteers should incorporate using volunteers to help individuals, families, children, and adults, not just tour groups. We should have "live" programs (classes, tours, etc.), but they should have lower priority than creating and maintaining gallery installations that help adult and family visitors benefit the most from their time in museum galleries. The new priorities for master teachers included researching collection areas for the purpose of teaching; creating interpretive materials for installation in the galleries; planning and implementing visitor research related to teaching people about the collections; and collaborating with curators on new ways to install collections so they are meaningful to visitors. These are not new tasks for educators. But the focus on independent visitors rather than live programs did feel like a revolution with all the attendant stress and strain one might expect. None of us can even imagine "going back," although we still struggle with having too much to do and with our more complex relationships with curators, designers, collection managers, and administrators.

SOURCES OF LEARNING

I looked at the last eight years, during which I've been the "master teacher for Asian art," and found five major sources of learning that have been critical to my professional growth. First are the words and thoughts from great minds:

■ Jonathan Spence's writing about the lives of individual human beings too often buried and lost in history, in this case the history of China

■ Stephen Addiss's accessible articulation of the aesthetic qualities and the cultural context of Japanese artworks in his *How to Look at Japanese Art*

■ Howard Gardner's *Frames of Mind, A Theory of Multiple Intelligences*, which describes my students, colleagues, and myself in ways that help me be a more thoughtful teacher

■ Keirsey and Bates's *Please Understand Me*, a practical book that helps me develop useful relationships with people who are temperamentally different than I am

The next three sources of learning are not very surprising: traveling to the countries that I teach about and seeing the real thing for myself; listening to what the kids I teach and the visitors we research have to say and integrating this into my own work; and watching and listening to my colleagues to find different ways to solve problems and deal with stresses at work. In the last area, the curator I work with the most, Ron Otsuka, and the two educators who share the duties of running the department, Gretchen DeScoise and Melora McDermott-Lewis, have provided lots of food for thought about the goals and projects we share.

Finally there is the most personal and intimate level of learning where some small, gradual, often stumbling changes come from learning about myself. In this area I like to have a good therapist on hand for times of stress or confusion. But I also have gone through a bout of breast cancer. There is no better stimulant for learning and change than a life-threatening illness. Since I had cancer surgery, and took time out from work for a delightful rest and full recovery, I've had a pretty clear vision of what I want to do next at work—more direct teaching with children while I maintain the teaching installations I've done with our Asian collections. Right now I'm still struggling with how to do this. But if I'm lucky I'll figure it out.

REVISITING CRITICAL ISSUES:
THE VIEW FROM A SEMI-RETIREE

by Zora Martin Felton

Four years have passed since my retirement from the Smithsonian's Anacostia Museum (now the Anacostia Museum and Center for African American History and Culture) in Washington, D.C. Since then I have been a faithful volunteer both in the museum and in the Anacostia community, serving on committees and boards and helping with special programs. I have served a six-month internship with the Smithsonian Archives on the Mall, and nearly two years volunteering in the Manuscript Division of Howard University's Moorland-Spingarn Research Center.

Former colleagues raise various issues of concern to museum educators: the "disconnect" among educators, researchers, and developers; limited human and material resources; the need for more training in museum management skills; assessments and evaluations; audience building; teaching and learning; new technology; competition among museums and between museums and popular entertainment entities; inclusiveness and diversity; museums as social instruments; and museum accessibility. The list goes on and on and on.

Obviously many issues have changed over the years; others, while called by slightly different names, remain to confound and frustrate us. I should like to briefly address two that may merit a second look: teaching and learning, and the museum as a social instrument.

TEACHING AND LEARNING

Recently, a retired public school teacher (who happened to be a teachers' college graduate) confided that one of the main reasons many children were failing in school was because their teachers were never taught how to teach. Dierking and Springuel bring this concern home to museum educators when they speak of staff who "have educator job titles but no formal training" as being among those who "still have much to understand about the learning process . . . the complex system of interactions between people and objects."

Years ago, the founding director of the Anacostia Museum, the late John Kinard, said that he wished to have a discussion with me about education in the schools: How do students learn? How do teachers teach? What are students learning? And how do teachers know what students are learning? My undergraduate secondary teaching certificate (long expired) was not sufficient for me to articulate answers that satisfied either of us. With his blessing I enrolled in the Howard University graduate school of education. I should also add that while working toward my M.Ed., I spent considerable hours in classrooms observing some of the most competent and effective teachers in the city.

Howard provided me with theory and a broad knowledge of the field of education. It further compelled me to reexamine the how and what and why, as I understood it, of museum education in a formal context. And interacting with the best and brightest teachers the system had to offer provided me with excellent role models and helped me solidify and adapt new techniques and approaches to learning in Anacostia.

All of this, of course, was before "new technology," especially computers, found its way into classrooms and homes. Educators are quick to point out that some approaches that might have worked well five or 10 years ago do not necessarily work now. Students, they say, want to interact in new ways. Others demand to be entertained. And they are vocal in expressing themselves. One museum educator told me of making changes in a program after students complained of being "tired of learning about dead people"; they wanted to know more about contemporary personalities.

As we move into the next century, it will be more and more difficult for museum educators to be effective without a thorough grounding in what EdCom has identified as "practice" in its *Goals 25* (1995) action plan. And the entire issue of teaching and learning in museums will continue to be a front-burner concern, if only because the whole field of education is ever changing and because our constituents both in the museum and in various collaboratives, partnerships, and other outreach settings have become more sophisticated and more selective in what, how, and why they wish to learn. How seriously we take the task of teaching and learning—as well as listening—will determine our chances for survival as a profession.

MUSEUMS AND SOCIAL RESPONSIBILITY

The issue of social responsibility and museums was deliberated decades before I entered the field. In my memory, however, it was raised repeatedly during the 1960s and beyond by many concerned directors and staff. During that period there were innumerable discussions and meetings during which thoughtful (and sometimes heated) dialogues took place as individuals struggled with what they considered a new definition of a museum's responsibility. As long ago as 1972, an AAM report entitled *Museums: Their New Audience* concluded that funding was "only the most painfully felt part of a larger crisis" that had to do with how museums were prepared to meet the challenge and opportunity of serving a new and diverse audience. The report recommended establishing various kinds of outreach centers or initiating community projects; sharing non-financial resources; reviewing hiring and training policies; and consulting with community groups in new ways.

But the report also recommended "high priority for exhibitions, acquisitions and programs relevant to current urban needs and problems, including as subjects, but not limited to, the population explosion, the environmental crisis, war, aging, disease, drug abuse, inter-group relations, and the histories of neighborhoods within the city."

As they say, those days are gone, possibly forever.

Within recent years, more and more museums have found it necessary to abandon the development of programs and exhibitions that veer from traditional museum fare usually found in the fields of art, science, and history. This trend has as much to do with funding and the dictates of present or potential donors as with philosophy. With regard to the latter, many of those same institutions are still quick to point out that the primary mission of the museum has nothing to do with its involvement with communities and their social concerns. The purpose of museums always has been and always will be to collect, preserve, exhibit, interpret, and provide opportunities for research. Period. And please, they say, do not question us about who collects, what is exhibited, and how things are interpreted.

However, contemporary voices like Edmund Barry Gaither maintain that "museums are ultimately human institutions. They belong to the body of institutional structures that communities created to serve perceived needs—to serve people. . . . What must follow is a diverse community of institutions that share responsibility for reshaping the world in which we will live." And Gaither is joined by others, such as Rex Ellis, who warns that we cannot "afford another monument to a small cultural elite that is in no way reflective of the people and times in which we live."

The Anacostia Museum was an early pioneer in showing how museums could successfully involve their communities by focusing on long-neglected urban concerns. "The Rat: Man's Invited Affliction" (1969), suggested and curated by education staff, explored the ecology of the Norway rat that then infested 85 percent of the Anacostia neighborhood. In describing this exhibit as well as a later one on drugs at the Museum of the City of New York, the AAM report declared that ". . . both dealt with subjects not previously thought of as within the scope of museum interests, but both were stunningly successful precisely because both did deal with aspects of the new life in the cities. Both were also, implicitly and explicitly, calls for social action of various kinds. Although some museums hesitate still to involve themselves in anything that might be so characterized, there is precedent for even passionate advocacy in the cause of, for example, better design of furniture and tableware, even though such demands were clearly against the immediate interests of commercial firms."

The Anacostia Museum followed the exhibition on rats with "Lorton Reformatory: Beyond Time" (1970). This exhibit, first suggested by the museum's custodian, took our staff to the city's penitentiary in northern Virginia. The purpose was to examine life behind the prison walls where numbers of Anacostia residents were then and still are incarcerated. So often did we visit that when the guards in the tower saw our blue jitney pull up, they would simply yell, "It's Anacostia again; open the gates!" Together, the museum's director, exhibits specialist, custodian, photographer, and two educators held planning meetings with residents inside the small schoolhouse. There, we jointly planned the exhibit and accompanying programs. Later, groups of Lorton men were escorted to the museum, where they helped mount the exhibit and, after the opening, returned as art and craft demonstrators and docents during the day, discussion leaders at night, and performing artists on weekends. Most often, weekends especially, our small museum was jammed with standing-room-only crowds.

To complete the exhibition trilogy, the museum opened "The Evolution of a Community: Part II" (1972). This show, the result of a neighborhood survey conducted by museum staff, focused on five urban problems identified by neighborhood residents: education, housing, recreation, drugs, and crime. In all three exhibitions, museum educators were involved in team efforts with all other staff in the museum.

While exhibition development is not ordinarily in the job description of today's museum educator, he or she can initiate programs that instruct, inform, and empower people to make thoughtful decisions about improving many aspects of their lives or the environments in which they live. They can, for example, as our staff did in 1994, organize a symposium on environmental justice. Ours focused on the Anacostia area and was attended by city officials, community residents, civic leaders, and others. As the discussions progressed, it was clear that once again Anacostia was a microcosm for many of the ecological ills that pervaded other inner-city jurisdictions such as ours. Many learned for the first time about local landfills, landslides, illegal dumping sites (used by outsiders who came in the dead of night), and, of course, the highly visible and polluted Anacostia River where, sad to say, many residents continue to fish.

As a follow-up to the discussions, staff and community members felt that they should develop an exhibition to tell yet another story of Anacostia. Using the land as a focus, current education staff determined they could bring together the disciplines of geology, geography, chemistry, physics, archaeology, and history. They could also weave into this the human element, not only telling the story of the dedicated neighborhood environmental activists who raise alarms and challenge city and federal officials, but also detailing the devastating psychological and physical effects of living in an unsafe and polluted environment. Unfortunately, to date the museum has been unable to find the resources to move forward with this project.

It is possible that, given the times and the temper of those who ultimately decide what the public will see in our museums, the day is long past when exhibitions will look beyond standard fare. If so, the loss will be as great to us as professionals as it will be to audiences who have a right to expect just a little bit more.

THE FUTURE

I believe that others presently in the field are far more qualified than I to speak about the future of the profession. But perhaps I might be allowed to offer thanks to so many who served as teachers and mentors to me: my colleagues, neighborhood residents, docents, teachers, the men who stood on our corner, and countless individuals—some with and some without formal learning. And always there were the children. Then, as now, as a volunteer reading aide in my neighborhood elementary school, I am continually inspired and renewed by their natural curiosity, beauty, and intelligence.

Had it not been for the children and the young people of the museum, there would never have been live rats in the rat exhibition. It was the youngsters who insisted that people who had never had a face-to-face encounter with rats should be able to see them up close in a simulated backyard environment. To John Kinard's credit, he allowed them to overrule understandably squeamish and apprehensive board members. The rest became history.

And had it not been for the children, three adults (two museum educators and a formally trained volunteer) would probably still be using pipettes to aspirate hundreds of ants—one by one—from a large trash bag. Our object was to transfer them into a gigantic ant farm in the museum's children's room. After inquiring about what we were doing, they sat quietly while we sucked, coughed, blew and sucked, coughed and blew some more. One then silently pulled a sheet of paper from her notebook and, without a word, placed the paper on top of the pile of dirt overrun with swarming ants. Immediately, more than 100 ants covered the paper and the child calmly shook them into the ant farm. Other children followed suit. It was then that the three professionals put down their pipettes and sheepishly asked to borrow sheets of paper from the children.

Crises come with the territory, although these days they do seem to appear more frequently and with greater intensity. Perhaps we as professionals need to more aggressively seek out those who can help us keep open minds and see things with unclouded eyes. Maybe there are still some people out there holding sheets of notebook paper who will point the way to new solutions and approaches to the challenges and changes around the corner.

REFERENCES

Dierking, Lynn D., and Springuel, Myriam, eds. "Current Issues in Museum Learning." *Journal of Museum Education* 16, no. 1 (Winter 1991): 3.

Ellis, Rex. "Museums as Instruments of Change." *Journal of Museum Education* 20, no. 2 (Spring/Summer 1995): 14-17.

Felton, Zora Martin, and Lowe, Gayle S. *A Different Drummer: John Kinard and the Anacostia Museum, 1967-1989*. Washington, D.C.: Anacostia Museum, Smithsonian Institution, 1993.

Gaither, Edmund Barry. "Museum Education and Ideals." *Journal of Museum Education* 16, no. 3 (Winter 1991): 9-10.

Goals 25: An EdCom Action Plan. Unpublished report. American Association of Museums Standing Professional Committee on Education, May 20, 1995.

Karp, Ivan; Kreamer, Christine Mullen; and Lavine, Steven D., eds. *Museums and Communities: The Politics of Public Culture*. Washington, D.C.: Smithsonian Institution Press, 1992.

Museums: Their New Audience. A Report to the Department of Housing and Urban Development by a Special Committee of the American Association of Museums. Washington, D.C.: American Association of Museums, July 1972.

Virshup, Amy. "Grading Teachers." *Washington Post Magazine*, Nov. 9, 1997, pp. 15-17 and 31-34.

———. "The Museum as a Social Instrument Revisited." *Journal of Museum Education* 14, no. 1 (Winter 1989).

———. Community Participation in Museums and Cultural Institutions. Unpublished report. Washington, D.C.: Anacostia Museum and Center for African American Culture, March 1997.

MUSEUM EDUCATION
IN TRANSITION

by Carolyn P. Blackmon

T here are three closely related critical issues that museum administrators and educators must consider if museum educators are to be fully equipped and prepared as practitioners in the arena of public education: career development and continuing education; community partnerships; and technological know-how. These are not new issues, but today they are in crisis. They are tied to both institutional mission and operation, including not only economics but clear position descriptions and appropriate salary schedules, hiring practices, performance reviews, fringe benefits, and guidance from local and national data. This 1982 quote forecast the issues discussed here—access to resources, quality programming, and the need for partnerships with formal education in communities and technology:

> The future of museum education hinges on many factors, but it
> can be no better than the quality of thought and vision brought to
> museum education. The self-fulfilling prophecy operates to the
> detriment of many museum education programs. If little is
> expected of educational programs, few resources are likely to be
> made available and the conscientious museum educator will be
> prevented from developing a program of high quality. . . . As an

agency for education the museum has inherited a number of
problems common to all institutions engaged in this endeavor.
The central problem is how to assure programming of high quality . . . there are some lessons for museum educators in the decline
of quality in public schools.[1]

In 1984, the Commission on Museums for the New Century addressed the
fabric and future of American museums as they neared the close of the 20th century. Four forces for change that would influence future choices for museums were
articulated: "many voices are demanding to be heard and involved in decision
making; cultural pluralism is expanding nationwide at a rapid rate; education is
expanding in the adult market; and high technology will have a significant impact
on our personal and museum lives." One of the commission's 16 recommendations
stated that "education is the primary purpose of American museums. To assure
that the educational function is integrated into all museum activities, museums
need to look carefully at their internal operational structures." Another said that
"we urge that museums continue to build on their success as centers of learning by
providing high-quality educational experience for people of all ages, but in recognition of the increasing median age of our population, that they pay new attention
to their programs for adults."[2]

The commission report asked that museums function not as a supplement
to schools but as institutions of equal status that embrace teaching and learning in
an informal setting that augments formal instruction. People continue to perceive
museums as elitist but museums hope audiences will see them as places to return
to again and again for enjoyment, learning, and use as a resource for exploration
and discovery. Community leaders are coping with such problems as the explod-
ing population, racial conflicts, and sad state of education in one Illinois suburb,
reported to the country by a respected group of leaders in 1997:

The boom years of the 1980's were as much a product of the luck
of location as they were of shrewd planning. Traffic is congested,
and mass transportation is substandard. DuPage is considered an

inhospitable place for newcomers who are something other than white. And the schools, although among the strongest in the state [Illinois], are not preparing students for employment. Those were the assessments of five of the region's most influential leaders in business, education and government at the conference, "Fast Forward—The Future," organized by the DuPage Area Association of Business and Industry.[3]

The opportunity has never been riper for museums to demonstrate their concern about these issues and strengthen their status by forming partnerships with leaders in cities and suburbs.

CAREER DEVELOPMENT AND CONTINUING EDUCATION

As museums pay more attention to visitors' interests and abilities, and as new definitions of "learning" emerge in museums, we need new kinds of expertise in the museum setting. The most obvious change has been in the development of "audience specialists"—the educators. But all other roles are changing, too, and becoming more specialized as technology/media, communication, and content and management responsibilities become more complex.

The National Science Foundation initiated a major reform for science education through a series of awards to state, urban, and rural school systems. The basic premise of each systemic initiative is that "all children can learn." A centerpiece of the awards focuses on training teachers who left academia eight to 30 years ago to re-enter the classroom. Information continues to accelerate at such a rapid pace that the axiom "nothing is as constant as change" is more relevant today than ever before. Museums share the same concerns as teaching and career development. Museum information may be more current for colleagues because they usually have academic support, but the need for continued refreshment is essential as we work with teachers, in teacher training, and in outreach programs, and as new school partnerships are formed, developed, and implemented.

In fact, museum educators are far more isolated from peers and resources in their work than schoolteachers. The need for continuing personal development demands a thoughtful solution that provides ongoing training programs to ensure a current and consistent syllabus that includes methodology and content. It is essential to bring new and veteran staff members up to a professional standard that matches the museum's desire for quality educational programs, performance expectations, and periodic reviews. Workshops and conferences are stimulating and provide an important networking function, yet they cannot always support individual needs and continuity of experience. When we look at the diversity of museums, their communities, resources, programs, and audiences, we see great enthusiasm and devotion mixed with an uneven landscape of professional background and expertise. Why does this happen? One reason is that museums often lack standard position descriptions and rarely conduct informative staff performance reviews. We say that collections and resources are the heart of a museum, its staff is its soul, and its audience is its reason for being. It is time to take a hard look at the health of its soul.

COMMUNITY PARTNERSHIPS

Many cultural institutions recognize a need and responsibility to serve diverse constituencies. This responsibility is more important than what is currently referred to as "market share." How does an institution position its staff and resources to serve its communities? The Field Museum, for example, has a 100-year history of outreach through an extensive school-loan program. But for a long time, we gave teachers what we thought was good for them rather than listening to their ideas, knowledge, and experience. To build program momentum and interaction and ensure that our educational programs remain relevant, we had to pay attention to our constituencies and visitors. Conversations with two eminent foundations helped us to recognize that we had to train museum educators to work with our teacher and community constituencies and to tackle new ideas and subject matter. Both initiatives resulted in publications designed to be training resources: *Teach the Mind, Touch the Spirit—A Guide to Focused Field Trips* and *Open Conversations—Strategies for Professional Development in Museums.*

Inter- and intra-institutional departmental planning is essential for identifying issues and establishing a productive working environment. Museums also can maximize their resources by collaborating with outside agencies and sister institutions. Some prerequisites for planning and implementation necessary for fruitful collaboration are based on the assumption that the museum's mission, goals, and objectives are clear regarding desired audience diversity and programming. Important prerequisites include activities to determine the need for collaboration and its effect on program goals; determine external and internal resources that can realistically satisfy additional demands on staff time, talent, etc.; examine financial resources required to adequately support an increased budget; identify goals in common with potential constituent organizations, e.g., colleges, universities, community organizations, public bodies, etc.; identify leaders within these constituencies—decision-makers and power bases; and develop a rationale for the program that clearly defines and articulates mutual benefits for collaboration, e.g., common goals, program augmentation, audiences to be served, expanded visibility to attract support, greater strength in collaborative efforts, cost savings, etc.

To accomplish this, museums should form an advisory committee and define clear roles and responsibilities for each participant. The committee should meet regularly to develop group goals and set a course of action, assign and follow up with sub-committees, and evaluate progress in a timely manner. A community group must take a leadership role in defining its needs and designating the group chairperson to work with museum staff member(s) responsible for planning and implementation. Too often the museum presents its program to a disinterested audience. It is also important to establish a feeling of camaraderie at the beginning of any collaboration. The museum should initiate this development. The museum's presence as listener and interested partner is essential. The primary goal is to develop mutual trust within a closely knitted partnership— museum and community. For example, the Field Museum is building a rich legacy of partnerships through research and educational programs that are historical, contemporary, and global. In turn, members of its continually expanding network know where they can seek advice and receive or locate assistance from institutions of similar size and interests.

Although, museums cannot solve social issues, they can provide a forum and a venue for discussion and, in an advisory role, provide appropriate and supportive linkages that encourage dialogue within the community and its networks.

TECHNOLOGICAL KNOW-HOW

Between 1950 and 1970 the number of computers in use grew from 15 to 100,000, mostly in businesses. Today computers are smaller and can be found in homes and schools, on trains and planes, together with cell phones, portable CDs, digital cameras, and other high-tech equipment. With this "knowledge economy" has come the need to know how to access and interpret information. The speed with which people can communicate and the quantity of information transmitted has transformed the workplace. Web sites are common and proliferating at a rapid rate. Webmasters have become a new and growing professional group who design most of the access points available to search. Museums should look to other industries for guidance as they build and rebuild databases of information and introduce new interpretive strategies for public learning. For example, according to the *New York Times*, " [a] Web site where travelers can book flights—and where the only semblance of fun involves mouse-clicking on continually updated plane charts to make seat selections—[was] expected to sell more than $100 million in airline tickets [last] year." A Microsoft executive noted, "We were romanced by the entertainment stuff, too. . . . But we underestimated the value of software. And you know there really is something very sexy about creating a product that is useful to people and can help them live their lives better."[4] Schools and museums also share the need for trained teachers with up-to-date knowledge, content, and resources. Currently, there is an attempt to marry video, CD-ROMs, and T.V. to explore technology in new formats. And then there is ELDLN, the Electronic-Long-Distance Learning Network. Illinois is taking "first steps in a plan to partly replace grade schoolers' clunky science textbooks with Web sites, interactive CD-ROMs, and the familiar voice of broadcast journalist Bill Kurtis," explains former Illinois Schools Superintendent Joseph Spagnolo. "I think this fills a tremendous void. Right now, kids don't learn science in school, they learn about it. The only way for kids to learn scientific principles is to see and touch them."[5]

We will soon greet the 21st century. The Class of 2002 has entered their freshman year and the Class of 2010 has entered first grade. The museum audience for the next century is being educated today. Museums can be instrumental in their education by creating and fostering new partnerships in their communities and schools as vital resources for students, parents, and teachers. The future is now.

REFERENCES

1. Laura H. Chapman, "The Future of Museum Education," *Museum News*, July/August 1992, p. 51.

2. Ellen Cochran Hirzy, ed. *Museums for a New Century: A Report of the Commission on Museums for a New Century* (Washington, D.C.: American Association of Museums, 1984).

3. T. Gregory, "Some see gaps in DuPage education," *Chicago Tribune*, Oct. 26, 1997.

4. A. Harmon, "At Microsoft, the Hip Gives Way to the Useful," *New York Times*, Oct. 13, 1997.

5. J. Manier, "Science Classes Set to Explore Web Potential," *Chicago Tribune*, Sept. 17, 1997.

ARTIFACTS AND ARTIFICTIONS

by Sally Duensing

Seeing Truth as made, not found—seeing reality as socially constructed—doesn't mean deciding there is nothing "out there." It
means understanding that all our stories about what's out
there—all our scientific facts, our religious teachings, our society's beliefs, even our personal perceptions—are products of a
highly creative interaction between human minds and the cosmos. The cosmos may be found; but the ideas we form about it,
and the things we say about it are made.

The Truth About Truth, edited by Walter Truett Anderson

A recent visit with a friend to the Museum of Jurassic Technology in
Los Angeles helped to connect some fragments of thought that have
been rattling around in my mind for quite a while on the nature of
what is significant, unique, and valuable in the overall educational
role of museums.

The Museum of Jurassic Technology is the creation of artist David Wilson.
Playing with the authoritative voice and traditional methods of museum presentation, Wilson has created exhibits that intentionally blur distinctions between real
and not real, juxtaposing everyday and exotic items. For example, there is an exhi-

bition about a fictional character, Geoffrey Sonnebend, a neurophysiologist who in a flash of inspiration created a theory that memory is an illusion. Forgetting, not remembering, was the inevitable outcome of all experience, according to the fictional Sonnebend. In addition to closely mirroring a traditional academic style, the exhibit was delightful and intriguing because its content had some interesting (and often humorous) perspectives that typify current theories on the constructive nature of memory.

The juxtaposition of the non-real Sonnebend with real, thought-provoking ideas is at the heart Wilson's vision. "Wonder, broadly conceived, is its unifying theme. Part of the assigned task, is to re-integrate people to wonder. The visitor continually finds himself shimmering between wondering at (the marvels of nature) and wondering whether (any of this could possibly be true). And it's that very shimmer, the capacity for such delicious confusion, Wilson sometimes seems to suggest, that may constitute the most blessedly wonderful thing about being human."[1]

Perhaps one of the most important educational roles a museum can play is to become an environment for generative inquiry. Rather than simply presenting artifacts or teaching scientific "truths," a museum can create an atmosphere in which exhibits present phenomena in such a way that they elicit new insights, questions, and wonder. The evocation of reflective and creative thought should be a major museum educational goal.

I've noticed two different ways of evoking wonder in museum settings. One kind creates awe in a remote or non-relational way with little personal connection or generative involvement. This type of response often occurs when seeing something with little context. Another kind of wonder actually draws you in and becomes part of you—or you become part of the experience—as in Wilson's exhibition about Sonnebend. In the book *Exhibiting Cultures*, Stephen Greenblatt refers to this kind of wonder as resonance: "A resonant exhibition often pulls the viewer away from the celebration of isolated objects and toward a series of implied half-visible relationships and questions."[2]

For example, Coco Fusco and Guillermo Gomez-Peña created a performance art piece to stimulate questions about the exoticism of the other in the use of living displays at world's fairs and cultural display techniques in natural history museums. Placing themselves in a cage in various galleries and museums as examples of a fictional tribe of Amer-Indians, they created costumes hybridized from ancient and contemporary Latino cultures and a fabricated history, including the habitation of a mythical place called Guatinaui, undiscovered by Columbus. "By representing the performance as 'authentic'—complete with documents giving detailed and 'informed' explanations to the public and presenting 'evidence' in the form of maps and texts which show specifically the location of Guatinaui—a fictional reality was constructed."[3]

An exhibition at the St. Louis Historical Society about the 1904 World's Fair provides a further example. Artifacts are juxtaposed with memories of 14 people who helped to create or worked at the fair. Their totally different perceptions of what the fair represented creates a broad perspective of realities in which one person's fact was another person's fiction.

Looking at processes of human perception provides another way to generate questions (and wonder) and has formed a foundation for my own interest and questioning regarding the relative nature of realities. The Exploratorium uses human perception as an interconnecting theme throughout the museum. As founder Frank Oppenheimer said, "The theme of human perception is fascinating and lively. The combination of detector, memory, calculator and manipulator that is utilized by sensory mechanisms to sort out what it real and unreal has many parallels in scientific investigation. It includes the admixture of the aesthetic and analytical judgments that is characteristic of good science. Furthermore, we believe that as people learn how they see, hear and feel, etc., they are also learning something about the way in which they make social and human judgments."[4]

For example, visitors learn how context can affect perception in the "Color Contrast" exhibit. The colors of squares appear to change as they are placed on backgrounds of different colors. In the "Eyewitness" exhibit, visitors watching a video enactment of a theft can compare their memories of what they saw, and then watch the video again to see what they remembered correctly. Discussions often follow on the veracity of memory. The exhibit environment becomes a focus of inquiry rather than a collective "right" answer, with the potential to create what the current director of the Exploratorium, Goéry Delacôte, calls a learner-driven environment.

The Maryland Historical Society and The Contemporary in Baltimore used the perceptions of artist Fred Wilson to reveal new insights into and new questions about the relations of artifacts and history. Unlike David Wilson, who mixes fact with fiction to reveal new truths and new questions, or Gomez-Peña and Fusco, who use complete fabrications of facts to reveal larger cultural truths about history and interpretation, Fred Wilson created an exhibition from the historical society's rich collection of objects, ranging from portraits and photographs to silver teapots and slave shackles. Using the museum's own processes and practices of display, Wilson looked at the relationship of what is on view and what is not on view to put a lens on ignored African-American and Native American history in Maryland.

In one gallery of the exhibition, "Cigar Store Indians turn their backs to the viewer and confront photographs of 'real' Indians. A label, 'Portraits of Cigar Store Owners,' implies the lumbering wooden figures tell us more about the stereotype held by their owners than about Native Americans."[5] Here, Wilson shows us that all artifacts are "artifictions." That is, both what we display and what we say about the things we display embody a multitude of possible interpretive narratives.

Involving a broader community is also a way to invite questioning and wonder. Wilson said that his own process of work underwent a profound change as a result of his interactions with various groups while creating the Baltimore exhibit. Rejecting the traditional role of the artist working alone, Wilson engaged all sorts of people in the process of the exhibit creation, including organizations as various and distinct as the Knights of Columbus and a local civil rights group. Wilson considers this process quite valuable, and said he would not have tried to do it before this exhibition.

Adding another voice to the exhibition were the perspectives of the visitors who attended the exhibit. "The notes visitors left on the exhibition response board sent a strong, unified message to our profession: museums are a place where visitors expect to have their views challenged and where they hope the museum will listen to their histories and welcome their perspectives. If museums are to be valued as institutions in the years to come, we must be attentive to our communities and the wider social contexts in which we operate."[6]

Visitor feedback has proven useful in other museum contexts as well. At the Ontario Science Center's provocative exhibit, "A Question of Truth," I watched people spend long periods of time reading and discussing other visitors comments about the exhibition and writing comments about other written comments. This exhibit uses perspectives of scientific evidence to look at ways cultures have interpreted astronomical events, health, and medicine, as well as racial and gender prejudices and biases both current and historical.

Visitor narratives can also become part of an exhibit. In the current Exploratorium exhibition on human memory, visitors are invited to contribute their earliest memories, associations with different smells, as well as ideas for what should go into a time capsule to help people in the future learn about our time. As I noticed in Ontario and in other exhibitions, visitors devote a great deal of time and thought to recording their own stories, and spend as much or more time reading what others have said.

In addition to exhibitry and visitor voice, the museum organization itself is a key ingredient for an educational mix that leads to inquiry. The museum's public learning environment can only be sustained if the internal culture also embodies that learning process. "Museums cannot become centers of learning unless they themselves also become learning organizations. For many museums this requires a change of organizational culture. Museum directors can lead this process in three ways: by publicly demonstrating their own commitment to education; by establishing structures for consultation and decision-making which open their institutions to debate and constructive criticism; and by encouraging and rewarding imagination, creativity, risk-taking and reflection."[7]

When he developed the Exploratorium, Frank Oppenheimer created a salon-like environment that encouraged colleagues from a variety of disciplines and communities to informally meet and work. These exchanges, ranging from a few hours to a few months, often resulted in intriguing new ideas and perspectives that would sometimes lead to unanticipated new programs or new exhibit ideas. For example, when the late poet Muriel Rukeyser was an artist in residence for several months to create a poetry and science reading series, discussions lead to the development of a proposal subsequently funded by the National Science Foundation for the creation of a new section of exhibits on perception and language.

These exchanges at the Exploratorium have evolved over the years into extremely influential programs for the ongoing formation of the museum. There are both occasional workshops with colleagues from other museums and a steady stream of formal and informal meetings with colleagues from a variety of fields. And there are now several annual, funded programs in which eight to 10 different people—artists, scientists, educators, anthropologists, etc.—are in residence for one month or longer to help us work on new ideas, new exhibits, and existing programs.

I have come to deeply appreciate and value a continual influx of outsider perspectives to both challenge and contribute to staff perspectives. This, of course, contributes to what is on the public floor. The artists, scientists, philosophers, educators, and anthropologists who were teachers and mentors for me in my initial museum work are also now part a continuously growing network of colleagues and friends from whom I continue to learn.

I believe that valuing multiple voices is crucial for keeping educational institutions alive as learning cultures. A museum can be a forum, a wonderful and often unique intellectual bazaar that encourages the sharing of multiple perspectives.

I am excited by the increasing willingness in many different kinds of museums to explore some of the new insights (and "shimmers of wonder") that can emerge from looking at objects, phenomena, or cultures in different contexts.

This interaction among human minds exploring the ideas—the artifacts and "artifictions" of our own understandings—are at the heart of what it means to be alive personally, professionally, and institutionally. Central to this process—and what has helped me through various crises of the nonprofit world—is the richness of inquiry that occurs when we encourage new ways of thinking and thus new ways of understanding.

Acknowledgment: I want to thank Ian Grand for the title, and Ian and Melissa Alexander for valuable comments concerning "Artifacts and Artifictions."

REFERENCES

1. L. Weschler, "Inhaling the Spore," *Harper's Magazine*, September 1994.

2. S. Greenblatt, "Resonance and Wonder" in *Exhibiting Cultures: The Poetics and Politics of Museum Display*, eds. Ivan Karp and Steven D. Lavine (Washington, D.C.: Smithsonian Institution Press, 1991).

3. C. Vercoe, "Postcards and Signatures of Place," *Art Asia Pacific* 3, no. 1 (1996).

4. F. Oppenheimer, Letter to Raymond Hannapel, National Science Foundation, 1971.

5. L. Corrin, "Artists Look at Museums, Museums Look at Themselves, The Maryland Historical Society" in *Mining the Museum: An Installation by Fred Wilson*, ed. Lisa Corrin (New York: The New Press, 1994).

6. G. Ciscle and C. Lyle, "Foreword" in *Mining the Museum: An Installation by Fred Wilson*, ed. Lisa Corrin (New York: The New Press, 1994).

7. D. Anderson, "Report to the Department of National Heritage" in *A Common Wealth: Museums and Learning in the United Kingdom* (London: Department of Natural Heritage, 1997).

CONVERSATIONS WITH COLLEAGUES

by Tessa Bridal

O nce upon a time, in the days of the Roman Empire, there was a lion who heard that an award was being offered to the beast who could consume the most Christians. The lion hurried to the Coliseum to compete. He was preparing to eat when one of his prospective snacks turned and whispered something in his ear. The lion cowered, backed away, and left the arena hurriedly. The lion was ordered to return and explain what the Christian had said to put him off his meal. "She explained," the lion said, "that if I won the award I would be expected to write a few words."

After seeing the names of the award winners who were invited to contribute to this publication, my sympathies were entirely with the lion.

I took courage from the fact that the cover letter inviting my participation said that "the emphasis is to have a variety of different voices and approaches to the subject." So I turned to several of my colleagues for inspiration. Before asking them to assist me with this essay, however, I felt it only right to ponder for myself the two questions we were asked to consider: "What do you see as the two or three critical issues facing professionals working today to make museums effective educational institutions?" And, "Whom are you learning from today—where are the future directions and the sources of your ideas?"

My thoughts led me to recognize that among my teachers are the physicists working on quantum mechanics, who suggest that whatever we study or observe, we change as a result of our observation. I have been observing museums for a number of years and both of us have changed as a result. This is not in any way unique to me. All of us who have participated in the life of museums have changed them.

Each time I read one of his books, I also learn from my countryman, writer Eduardo Galeano, who says: "We are what we do, especially what we do to change what we are."

My passion for education stems from a life experience that taught me that the fight for change is worth fighting even when it's lost, because the fight itself inspires others. This experience suggests that when we fight for change, losing is not even a possibility.

One of the changes I worked to bring about in museums was a programmatic approach that included using theater to encourage discussion on topics such as sexism, religious bigotry and persecution, medical ethics, and environmental issues; and the development of science demonstration programs that emphasized the thrill of discovery and the processes of science. I have worked to encourage museums to capitalize on what theater does best: transform spaces, ideas, and, ideally, ways of thinking, by inviting audiences to encounter and grapple with ideas.

One of my greatest challenges is well expressed by Carol Shively in her article, "Get Provoked" ("Applying Tilden's Principles," in the July/August 1995 edition of *Legacy*). "Information, as such," Shively writes, "is not interpretation. Interpretation is revelation based upon information."

Another of my challenges is well expressed in AAM's 1991 report: *Excellence and Equity: Education and the Public Dimension of Museums*. The report said that "museums can no longer confine themselves simply to preservation, scholarship, and exhibitions independent of the social context in which they exist. They must recognize that what we are calling the public dimension of museums leads them to perform the public service of education—a term we use in its broadest sense to include exploration, study, observation, critical thinking, contemplation, and dialogue."

Taking this to heart, it would follow that we, as educators, would first need to educate ourselves about the "social context" of our exhibitions. This would mean examining what the exhibition means to us personally; to the various communities to which we belong (spiritual, ethnic, gender, or age specific); to the larger community of which we are a part (city, state, or national); and to the global community. Such an examination could encourage us to broaden our own and one another's interpretations by fostering discussion and observation. It could also make the exhibition relevant to our visitors.

Assuming that we can then find commonalities between what we are exhibiting and those for whom we are exhibiting it, we can dwell on any aspect we choose or examine difficult social, economic, and environmental issues.

In "Arts Education for a Lifetime of Wonder," E. Gordon Gee and Constance Bumgarner Gee of Ohio State University write: "As a society, we would never think it adequate merely to 'expose' students to math or science. But in the arts, we think exposure—a trip to see *The Nutcracker* or a visit to the art museum—can substitute for sustained study of the arts. . . . Exposure is not education, information is not knowledge, and access is not comprehension."

When I asked my colleagues to comment on the critical issues facing professionals working to make museums effective educational institutions, I received a variety of responses. Ruth Thompson, head of special exhibits for the Science Museum of Minnesota, said that exhibits increasingly appear to cater to the lowest common denominator, what she referred to as "the dumbing down of America." She worries about our reluctance to address difficult, serious issues with our exhibits, offering "sound bite education where we experience the exhibit but don't learn anything." Thompson expressed concern about museums' increasing reliance on special project funding and about the lack of internal support for the institution's educational mission.

This concern was shared by our neighbor Gordon Murdock, curator of education at the Bell Museum, who observed that museums' public utterances seem less and less about their substance (their collections and history) and more and more about their social role: "We seem to be moving away from teaching about our subject areas, such as natural history, to teaching about how our institutions work." Murdock asked whether, when we teach classes about diorama or exhibit design, it's at the expense of the content and subject matter of the exhibits in question. Like Thompson, Murdock also talked about how fund raising takes up more and more time. He expressed concern that funding sources may set the agenda for an institution. The funder's goals may be fine ones, but were they the institution's goals before it learned that money was available to fund them?

Murdock added that more and more is being asked of those of us who work in museums, often meaning we have less time for professional development. Wendy Ellefson, interpretive programs supervisor at the Minnesota History Center, seconded Murdock by saying that while educators want to embrace technology and its tools, we often feel that with each new tool that comes along, technological expectations and standards are set higher and higher. These new tools and technologies must not only be used effectively, they must be maintained and updated at an increasingly fast pace.

Presenting another view of this issue, Nancy Fuller, research program manager at the Center for Museum Studies of the Smithsonian Institution, identifies the lack of technology capabilities in museums as one of the great challenges facing museum educators. Fuller sees technology as "a democratizing tool" that many museums are not sufficiently driven to use.

Another Minnesota neighbor, David Reese, executive director of the Bakken Library and Museum, expressed his concern about making sure that we "explain that what we do has some value to society. Museums are intermediaries between the academic world and the public. Translating the scholarship behind our collections" is an important focus.

Stewart Miller, executive director of the Thomasville Cultural Center in Georgia, agrees. Miller wants his audiences to understand "that folk art is accessible, something almost anyone can do, yet requiring skill."

Lyndel King, director and chief curator of the Frederick R. Weisman Art Museum at the University of Minnesota, said that one of her great challenges is to "translate critical thinking about works of art into critical thinking about other images."

Wendy Ellefson spoke of her frustration at having limited resources and few benefits to attract and sustain a corps of qualified employees. "Interpreters," Ellefson said, "often comprise the largest class of employees at museums and historic sites. Administrators and the general public have standards and expectations for this group that are getting higher and higher." Yet this element, representing and embodying the museum's public face, has skills that rarely translate into commensurate salary levels—typically, they are among the lowest paid staff at the museum. Although interpreters are highly valued as the institution's public representatives, the cost of a human presence in exhibits relegates these positions to part-time and temporary status.

After spending considerable time talking to my generous colleagues about these issues, I reached the by-no-means-extraordinary conclusion that museums are in transition, which, as any mother knows, tends to be the most difficult part of labor. In successfully transforming ourselves from places of static exhibitry to dynamic and interactive program spaces using the tools of both the education and entertainment industries, we have given birth to a demanding and challenging child.

As Walt Whitman said: "It is proven in the essence of things that from any fruition of success, no matter what, shall come forth something to make a greater struggle necessary."

MOVING BEYOND
THE MILLENNIAL TRANSITION

by Susan Bass Marcus

The current trend among museum professionals is to obsess about the 21st century. Where is this leading us? We know that considerable changes have taken place in the field of museum education in recent decades. They attest to a major shift in institutional priorities. Yet as the new century approaches, a profusion of stories in print and other media have been encouraging us to couch our long-range planning discussions strictly in terms of the new millennium. Given the great strides the field has made to date, museum professionals should regard the millennial transition not as the gateway to some radically new world, but as an opportunity to promote innovation while guarding lessons from the past.

My own childhood encounters with Chicago museums provided stimulating and informative experiences that shaped my development and implementation of programs at Spertus Museum, a major component of Spertus Institute of Jewish Studies in Chicago. As a museum educator, I am actualizing my youthful fantasy of spending countless hours in just such a place. Spertus Museum's exhibits, programs, and mission focusing on Jewish history and cultures resonate with my own identity and personal goals. Nevertheless, I find myself face to face with the coming century, and I find that now and then I must remind myself how the power of great exhibits and intriguingly planned museums spaces has affected me deeply over the years. Otherwise, like the enormous megalith from Stanley Kubrick's film, *2001*, this specter of century future will overshadow my professional common sense and sensibility, whether I am considering mission statements, museum visitors, exhibit design, institutional publishing, or funding.

The administrators, curators, and department heads of Spertus Museum meet often to reevaluate the design and impact of the museum. While not gathering expressly to confront the 21st century, we feel its challenge intensely in the course of our recent discussions. The institution is dedicated to the intellectual, cultural, and spiritual legacy of the Jewish people. Logically, the millennium—rooted in Christian philosophical and calendrical concerns—ought to have little bearing on a Jewish museum's long-range planning. To the contrary, among our institutional concerns is the preservation of Jewish heritage: We have the responsibility to put forward and interpret the past in terms that will appeal to museum participants, now and for generations to come.

Regardless of that commitment, the impending turn of the millennium stokes our imaginations with images of promise and renewal. "Planning for the 21st Century"—a slogan that alludes to creativity and a definitive break with the past—has a certain ring to it. Moreover, anyone who creates museum education programs or designs exhibits knows the pressure to keep abreast of current trends and new techniques, the latest research and up-to-date strategies. All this innovation and revision, however, should help us meet the needs of the people we serve with the resources we have preserved and interpreted, and not be simply "the greatest with the latest."

While the millennial transition is, indeed, a shibboleth of our time, it is also a chimera. Well before talk of the new millennium intruded into staff meetings, perceptive museum educators were developing imaginative and resourceful practices. Research, dedication, and ingenuity are evident, for example, in publications such as the Association of Youth Museums' *Hand to Hand* or *The Museum Education Roundtable* and in the rise of new definitions of museums. The phenomenon of the contemporary children's museum is one illustration of how much museums have changed in the last 50 years, especially by challenging the definition of "museum" and putting the word "interactive" into every museum educator's vocabulary.

This notion of a children's museum has had far-reaching effects on the aims of other more traditional and collection-based institutions. For example, in 1987, Spertus Institute of Jewish Studies (then Spertus College of Judaica), was spending considerable time and thought on ways to reach more people from diverse backgrounds. During this process of self-assessment and reinvigoration, plans for the Paul and Gabriella Rosenbaum ARTiFACT Center took root. Referring to the children's museum model, the center's planning committee hired an independent consultant to design a new interactive gallery that would teach about Jewish heritage in terms accessible to Chicago-area schoolchildren. The consultant was one of the original designers of ExpressWays (today, three locations and versions later, the Chicago Children's Museum) and sensitive to the ways that children become enthusiastic about learning. She recognized that ancient history is a daunting subject that becomes more interesting if placed in the context of an archaeological dig. Accordingly, the core piece of the new museum gallery was a tell, a dig site shaped like a mound. It would provide several digging stations representing about 1,400 years of Jewish history. Fragments of real ancient artifacts or copies of objects in Spertus's collection of antiquities would constitute the "finds" in each station or trench. ARTiFACT Center staff would teach archaeology techniques to the public and help visitors understand their discoveries. With the intention of recreating the historical setting of those artifacts, the designer proposed the Marketplace, a circle of learning stations that would surround the tell; each "booth" would explore an aspect of daily life in Israel 3,000 years ago.

I joined the development team in 1988 and worked closely with the designer to create the content and "feel" of the exhibition. My contribution supported the museum's original goals for the ARTiFACT Center by establishing a family education center; by giving visitors additional insights into Jewish heritage; and by raising the institution's public profile. Very soon after opening to the public in 1989, the ARTiFACT Center surpassed two of those goals.

The effect of good publicity, generous funding, and the center's sound educational and entertainment values was that our audience grew rapidly within our first year. We attracted families and some school groups representing a wide range of grade levels. Teachers jumped at the chance to take this new and unusual field trip, although some of them brought their classes seemingly without integrating the tour into their curriculum. Nevertheless, like nervous producers on opening night, we were thrilled about our "great" reviews. Kindergartners and eighth-graders alike entered the center with expressions of wonder or delight.

In the early 1990s, we noticed a change: More and more sixth-grade teachers were bringing their classes to us. In Illinois, then and now, the sixth-grade social sciences curriculum included a unit on ancient civilizations. Teachers discovered that Spertus Museum provided them with a unique and engaging way to enhance and augment their curriculum, a phenomenon for which we hoped, prayed, and prepared. Some of them already were implementing an archaeology-based curriculum, and they told me that a trip to the ARTiFACT Center was the perfect complement. The ARTiFACT Center's two-hour tour fit their curriculum, as a point of departure or as the culmination of their unit on ancient civilizations.

Eventually, we could no longer accommodate all the requests for tours of the dig. The museum tour coordinator and I had to address the pressure that sixth-grade teachers put on our scheduling. In less than 4,000 square feet of exhibit space, with a small staff of volunteers and professionals, the center could accommodate only a limited number of middle-school tour groups. We responded to the growing demand by limiting early childhood tour groups. We focused more and more on the curriculum needs of middle-school teachers and their students: Our discussions and exhibits echoed and explored the ancient civilizations that students were learning about in school. In fact, before its galleries closed temporarily, the Oriental Institute at the University of Chicago partnered with us. School districts would send us their entire sixth grade. As students spent a day on our two campuses, they learned about the discovery and collection of artifacts in the context of both their original setting and as the objects of study and display. I was delighted that our exhibits and programs were attracting a significant portion of our targeted audience.

Coupling this development with other innovative programs and workshops, I thought, we had addressed the most pressing needs of our public. However, the increasing number of families who brought their younger children during our public hours and the many adults who began to visit the ARTiFACT Center gallery on their own encouraged us to reexamine the dimensions of our programming.

During this period of changing priorities and reassessment of the ARTiFACT Center, my staff and I explored several other museums that used a variety of communication strategies and exhibits. A combination of simpler and more complex text labels, illustrations, interactives, and artifacts on display gave the visitor a choice of paths to follow or disregard. With such models in mind, my staff and I set out to rework two of the Marketplace spaces that would respond to visitors' curiosity about certain aspects of daily life in ancient Israel and appeal equally to adults and children.

Our recent efforts have been successful. The newest permanent exhibition, "Music in the Marketplace," focuses on ancient Middle Eastern music and instruments. More than 20 sound-producing interactives, text labels, illustrations, and a "make it-take it" station combine to make the music of the ancient world (with an emphasis on Israel) come alive. Although this area has proven to be very attractive, second only to the dig itself, we learned from watching and listening to visitors and a consultant that we needed exhibit modifications in some areas for clarity and accessibility, such as lowering labels and interactives. We learned from this latest enterprise that visitors participate idiosyncratically in an exhibition. Their previous experiences, curiosity, need for wonder and amusement, and available time influence the outcome of their encounter with our construct. Consequently, we intensified our evaluation process to understand visitors' needs and reconcile them with our institution's goals.

The second new permanent Marketplace exhibition, "The Oasis," which opened in the spring of 1998, demonstrates the lessons we have learned from the past. Both exhibits also reflect an important factor that produced the excitement I felt in the museums of my childhood— they provide the magic of an immersion experience. "The Oasis," for example, carries the visitor back to Israel and the site of our tell 2,500 years ago, with palm trees; an ancient desert water hole; *trompe l'oeil* murals of the Judean hills; reproductions of food, clothing, household appurtenances, toys, and equipment of that time; many engaging interactives; and a few text labels. The exhibition offers what I love in museums—a secret portal into a wonderland.

After nearly 10 years at Spertus Museum, I have felt the impact of several influences on our planning and design, the least of which is millennial fever. The latter might accelerate an amazing array of technological innovations, but we won't have a *Star Trek* "holodeck" for quite some time. Instead, here and now, and not in the Gamma Quadrant, museum visitors will pursue their own journeys in our galleries, in our immersion setting of re-creation and self-discovery. They will linger where an intriguing and absorbing environment introduces artifacts and activities that offer another perspective on those experiences.

The future will continue to challenge us at Spertus Museum. Although we are committed to preserving the past and to interpreting it in terms of the present, we are charged with transmitting it to future generations. The next century will bring plenty of changes, and we will need to be prepared for new terms, new definitions, and new perceptions. Dedicated to the story of the Jewish people, Spertus Museum will continue to encourage reflection on the meaning of our journey even as we travel beyond the millennial transition.

LOOKING TOWARD THE FUTURE

by Susan Bernstein

I f there were really only two or three critical issues facing museum educators as we head into the next century, we would be able to concentrate our efforts, pull in our reins, and charge ahead. Typically hard-working museum education professionals would produce long- and short-range plans with itemized budgets and detailed timelines. All of this drafted by the stroke of midnight on Dec. 31, 1999. No, not drafted, but finalized. The document would probably include a plan for improving the museum staff's communication with those outside its walls and with each other, increasing partnerships, and improving organizational performance.

Our association conferences and professional journals are making us keenly aware of the many issues to be discussed as we reflect on the next millennium. The American Association of Museums' list of "challenges and opportunities" museums face over the next three years presents 16 statements as a start (*Museum News*, September/October 1997, pages 67-68). Seven directors of major natural history museums provided seven different perspectives when they discussed the challenges and strategies of the 21st century (*Museum News*, November/ December 1997, pages 39-49). As we move closer to the year 2000, we become more introspective as a profession, and I think we can honestly say that the list of critical issues is long and getting longer.

These lengthy lists tell us much about who we are now. They also prompt us to consider our shortcomings as educational institutions. We certainly haven't done enough to forge a connection between our missions and those we want to serve. We haven't responded well enough to the demographic and cultural changes in our audiences. Our ability to increase income through new funding sources has not increased at the same rate as our ideas for how to use this money. Decision-makers are questioning our tax-exempt status and at the same time demanding more from us. All this points to much work ahead.

COMMUNICATION WITH PEOPLE OUTSIDE MUSEUMS

A critical issue museums face is how to better communicate our value to society. There are probably more people who don't know the purpose of our existence than people who do know. Educators are in a unique position because they can demonstrate the museum's work as an educational institution and the value that it serves in our society. We can be leaders in communicating what we are and how important that is. Museums house resources that help us understand and appreciate our cultural and scientific legacy. Collections gain added meaning through scholarship, research, exhibits, and educational programs. This helps us understand more about what it means to be human.

Long ago staff of museums were successful when their collections were well curated and there was a steady stream of acquisitions. This has changed. Our value is determined by how well we serve the public through our work. Our mission statements place a greater emphasis on education and public service. The University of Alaska Museum in Fairbanks has a mission statement written specifically for its education department. This has provided strong grounding for the staff and has undergone several revisions as the museum and times change. It is a road map that helps them move ahead in a positive and proactive manner.

Communicating the value of philanthropy is one of our social responsibilities, especially when we balance demands for expanding services with decreasing financial support. The public is in a quandary about whether to support museums and to what extent. People loudly ask what they will get in return. In delivering the lesson that giving to museums helps our community improve, we need to start with young people. For example, a membership officer at the San Diego Museum of Man encouraged student memberships by developing a lesson on philanthropy, then sending students' thank-you letters and drawings to members, donors, and government offices.

Much of what is regarded as better communication reflects the marketing-specialist role educators are asked to perform. Like cultural anthropologists, they need to understand the culture of museum program participants. We must know where participants live, their specialized interests, what hours are best for taking classes, how much they will spend on workshops, and much more. Changes in demographics and technology and the increase in a global economy pressure us to think differently about our audiences. How will they spend their time and their money in educationally enriching areas? We wonder about their prior museum experiences. The rapid turn towards visitor evaluations (focus groups, visitor surveys, interviews, demographic studies, and behavioral studies) all say to our audience: You are our partner; you are important to us. The clear message is that the more we can learn about who you are, what your needs are, and what you want from us, the better we will be able to serve you.

Once we're confident we've started to understand our visitors and what they want, we will be faced with an important challenge: to be(come) or not to be(come) consumer driven. We are effective at designing learning opportunities that allow visitors to explore or discover our institution's resources while demonstrating what the museum wants people to know about anthropology, art, history, or science. Evaluation results can guide us to what the visitor wants to know about our subjects. An issue to consider is how we balance and strengthen who we are with this demand.

To be more than we are now is a great pressure. "Make it more fun," we hear, or "bring in more money." "Bring in more people" or "make it more relevant." Being more doesn't just happen. It is planned for carefully by vision, management, and review. A well-thought-out five-year plan developed by the San Diego Zoo educators and facilitated by an outside consultant has been their strategic tool for growth. What we are not hearing enough from our directors and board members is "What do I need to do to help you—the leader of our museum's educational efforts—be more?"

To be more effective leaders, we need to look closely at how we communicate with each other. The style of communication within the institution is very similar to how the institution communicates with its audiences. When I wander through a museum that really invites me to participate, I think (and hope) that the behind-the-scenes communications among staff departments and with administrators is similarly professional and creative. We have all experienced difficulties in building constructive inter- and intra-departmental communication. Weekly meetings and semi-annual retreats help a great deal. Establishing employee grievance policies and exit interviews will help give and get feedback. It is important that museum professionals make each other honestly aware of objectives, shared values, and problems.

How do we communicate in difficult situations, especially when we don't always participate in the decisions about what and how information is given to the public? Educators should play a critical role in developing the process and content of exhibitions. Our unique perspectives and backgrounds help tremendously in this process. More than offering programs once the exhibit opens, we must contribute at the beginning of the process. We know our audience, and we know how to articulate educational "take-home" messages. We need to be advocates for our audience to the rest of the staff.

If our staff, administrators, and board members value different opinions and viewpoints, can we communicate with each other, share visions, solve problems, and plan for the future? When faced with a crisis (e.g., decreasing attendance, significant drop in membership, cancellation of a major annual fund raiser), can the institution develop a strategy and implement it with staff, administrators, and board members without thwarting the team? It is constant work to consistently employ a management style that is engaged in continuous improvement.

COLLABORATIONS/PARTNERSHIPS

Broadly speaking, the community is our partner. More specifically, we have opportunities to develop partnerships and collaborations with other not-for-profits, businesses, and government. We need to set up new non-traditional partnerships as well as work more closely with museums and other nonprofits in local, regional, state, and national efforts that promote our value in our communities. It helps our effectiveness to set up mutually advantageous partnerships. How many skeletons of exploitative partnerships hang in our closets after decisions were made only for the betterment of our institutions? I have heard too many times how grateful "they" should be for working with "us."

Why are collaborations/partnerships so important to us? They help us expand our capabilities and our mission. An institution with few staff and a small budget can produce more through collaborations and partnerships than alone. We can juggle more projects and venture out into new territories. The San Diego Museum of Man and the San Diego Opera worked on a jointly sponsored lecture and ended with a series of lectures, a symposium, two receptions, and a traveling exhibition to complement the world premiere of the opera, *The Conquistador*. The synergy of working together motivated us to expand and move in new directions. Sharing the work and combining our expertise helped us understand how much stronger we became when working interdependently.

We face the emerging responsibility of being key negotiators for collaborations and partnerships and often have the most vested in understanding and working with the museum's audience. We need to work with management and board members to place greater priority on building partnerships by demonstrating our successes and our willingness to learn from mistakes. We must learn how to brainstorm with newcomers outside our field and new partners from various museum departments. This could change how we do our job, and it could make doing our job a lot easier.

We must become integrally involved as partners with the formal education community. If we are not being asked to participate in discussions regarding national and state standards, textbook selection, assessments, and teacher training, we need to find a place at the table. It is critically important for us to be up-to-date on the concerns and changes in educational pedagogy. Teachers' relationships with museum resources are important for working interdependently, and there needs to be a higher priority placed on teacher training and developing partner projects.

We have much to offer as partners with the formal education community. The skills we teach for learning in a museum (observation, questioning, critical thinking, intuitive thinking, feeling and articulating, "reading" an object in context) are very important in an individual's lifelong education. They help us retain and apply information, encourage us to learn more, problem solve, and approach new challenges with more confidence.

MANAGEMENT/ORGANIZATIONAL PERFORMANCE

Our ability to increase organizational performance is critical for becoming more effective educational institutions. Museums are becoming ever more complex to manage. We are working to expand services as personnel, funds, and space decrease. We must sometimes eliminate older but successful programs in order to develop new initiatives.

Some recent developments in education theory emphasize participatory learning, and even the more traditional museums are looking for ways to create hands-on or "minds-on" experiences. The hands-on experiences concerning a cultural group in an exhibit, a non-threatening and humanistic environment, can provide visitors with a personal and long-lasting understanding. The replicated 18th-dynasty Egyptian home in "Time Travel to Ancient Egypt" at the San Diego Museum of Man exemplifies this. These experiences create cultural awareness, appreciation for diversity, and the ability to build connections and recognize commonalities among people. Museums have a social responsibility to address cross-cultural topics in order to promote intercultural understanding. Through interactive exhibitions about cultures, children and their parents can learn about what it means to be human, our needs, and the various ways to meet these needs.

There is an increased demand to keep up with and use technology in all aspects of our programs and operations. The obstacles to doing so are very real:

diminishing funds for purchasing equipment and lack of time and money for adequate staff training. It is also very important to use technology in new and interesting ways rather than in the same old ways. Will we be able to post summaries of books written by curators, notes by guest speakers, and labels from the current exhibit on our Web sites? Will our collections be accessible by a database search engine on the Web? Could voice-recognition technology help visitors pronounce artists' names or cultural items? Will we produce annual CD-ROMs on our temporary exhibits? If we don't, Microsoft will.

We need to use technology in new ways to help us become more effective in managing educational functions. A database of members and participants in education programs could help us personalize our communication with members. If we knew who visited the newly opened Maya ceramics exhibit, attended a lecture on pre-Columbian art, and purchased a *huipil* (a woman's sleeveless blouse made on a backstrap or treadle loom) from our shop, we could customize invitations to join a museum expedition to visit archaeological sites in Mexico. We could ask for follow-up, give post-visit or event suggestions, and provide an individualized study guide for personal educational exploration.

Educators will be catalysts for change and leaders in facing future challenges. We must continually convince other staff, management, board members, and the general public that museums are educational institutions and that the kind of learning that takes place in them is unique and a complement to the learning that takes place elsewhere.

FUTURE DIRECTIONS AND SOURCES OF MY IDEAS

I look to many places for future directions and sources of ideas. In the electronic media I see reports I might not happen upon in the libraries, or I follow my museum colleagues' discussion of recent issues on Museum-ed. We can peruse the information reports disseminated by the U.S. Department of Education's Office of Educational Research and Improvement, such as *Building on What We've Learned: Developing Priorities for Education Research, 1996.* This report stresses the importance of building links in our community for early education, schools, adult education, and corporate job training. It considers what constitutes quality out-of-school cultural activities, what constitutes equitable access to these activities, and the factors that contribute to success of high quality out-of-school learning.

As an anthropologist, I'm always reading new books about the human situation from evolution to contemporary social issues. Recently, I have been reading Jared Diamond's books: *The Third Chimpanzee*; *Guns, Germs, and Steel*; and *Why Is Sex Fun?* These are well-written overviews of our biological and cultural evolution by a knowledgeable scientist, with examples that give an understanding of our human identity. My personal interest is in applied anthropology and I read two journals, *Anthropology Today* and *Cultural Survival*. These offer examples and explanations about our changing world. They point to social responsibilities that give me future ideas for exhibits and programs.

Drawing new ideas from an array of resources will add to our future direction, helping us describe a vision for ourselves and our institutions. We should bring in new partners and widen our educational objectives with programming on philanthropy and on intercultural understanding. But the good that we are doing can't stay a secret among a small group of insiders. Essential to our mission will be communicating our value to those within and outside our institutions. We must step out as effectual leaders with vision and productive management. We have many mentors and supporters to help us along the way. Add to this ingenuity and determination, and we should be ready to take on the challenge of successfully moving into the millennium.

CHOICE AND AUTHENTICITY

by Barbara Moore

In the preparatory phase of a 1990 exhibition featuring a decade of work by the contemporary artist Robert Morris, the issue of how—or whether—his pieces might be interpreted was handled through various communiqués. Morris, who is also an eloquent writer and essayist, had penned a rather long letter that winter describing his view of the museum educator, which, in the case of that exhibition, was me. Essentially, he argued, the museum educator is the "voice" of the object, and, as such, has the power to control what a visitor thinks of the art on view. When I saw Morris's single-spaced, three-page declaration, which included a touching account of how he experienced art in his formative years, I had two reactions: One, my head was on the block. And, two, I had a chance, if I could handle the anxiety involved, to interpret the work of a living artist with exquisite sensitivity to the seriousness of purpose and immediacy of influence that defines museum education. I researched Morris like a demon and wrote a brochure that I hoped carried a few well-chosen areas of discussion to the reader walking through the exhibition. I am happy to say that things worked out. Morris reviewed the brochure's draft copy after it was vetted by the exhibition curator, and his changes were mainly an elimination of his name in favor of increased focus on his work. In the end, I was a guest at a small dinner held the night the exhibition opened, invited at the artist's request.

CHOICE

Now, as the reader of this piece, are you asking yourself why I recount this self-serving tale? It is because I have been asked to write to my colleagues on the issues I feel we face in our profession as museum educators, and to comment on the sources I look to for my own preparation of interpretive work. In the case of the Morris exhibition, I am convinced that by making choices I passed the test and produced something for the public that also seemed right to the artist. And so I place myself on record to say that I believe *choice is a central issue in museum education.* Regardless of the cliché it embodies and the disdain it can elicit among museologists, ours is the information age. Who will make sense of it, if not the museum educator? Woe to the visitor trying to appreciate a collection or exhibition saddled with a suite of informational bells and whistles, each one calling out for attention. Imagine (you probably don't have to) that poor visitor's cluttered "world of learning opportunities," created without the advantage of judicious, subject-related, and audience-sensitive choice: the computer's "virtual preview," the wall texts, the film, the brochure, the studio module. Choice calls us. Definitely.

In my view, choice is usually demanding, sometimes vexing. Before making it, you have to absorb lot of material. Then you must consider for whom you are choosing. Are you bristling now over what gives me the right to choose for others, including you if you happen to visit a museum where I am toiling away behind a wall? Yes, this is a temptation to bolt from the road of choice. So I will add another belief directly related to choice: Educators get to choose because their training has prepared them and their experience has seasoned them to make beneficial judgments about content and its usefulness in the museum setting. Also, it is their responsibility. Educators have backgrounds relevant to the subjects they interpret. Educators have access to the most current scholarship in the area they undertake to interpret. Educators are in touch with museum visitors; know the audience profile of their museums; have read and participated personally in audience evaluations; are familiar with different types of learning that occur in their museum. Educators are the ones who have to say, "This information, presented in a particular way or ways, will support my museum's visitors in their experience of art."

Educators also get to choose, or at least express a preference for, the forms of delivery that a particular interpretation might take in order to maximize its usefulness. Frankly speaking, the form of educational initiatives is sometimes more contested than its content as a result of aesthetic concerns, practical constraints, and the like. Still, the educator's expressed choice of delivery is an essential component of effectiveness. Do you want to communicate information about a popular show through individual explanatory wall labels when you anticipate huge crowds? I remember one exhibition, "A New World: Masterpieces of American Art, 1760-1910," representing 150 years of American painting and 40 of the country's most beloved and challenging artists from John Singleton Copley to Winslow Homer and Thomas Eakins, which premiered at the Corcoran Gallery in 1984. Sustained interpretation of the kind that requires reading in the galleries was determined a bad idea. Instead, labels with the most basic information—artist, and name and date of painting—were installed in giant-size type way above the heads of anticipated visitors to the show. Do you feel like screaming, "Oh, the horror, the horror . . ." in homage to Joseph Conrad's *Heart of Darkness*? When the anticipated crowds did appear, in waves that remained unabated until the last hour of the show's duration had passed, visitors told anyone who would listen how great it was to have large labels they could read in the press of bodies moving through the galleries. There were interpretive programs carried out in the museum's auditorium and workshops, but you get the point.

AUTHENTICITY

It's one thing to deal with crowds and icons, another to handle incendiary material. Here, a different kind of choice obtains, often independent of practical issues of crowding or theoretical issues of learning styles and audience profiles, yet more deeply embedded in museum policy. When faced with a subject around which fierce debate is inchoate or existent, *choice is inextricably bound to perspective*. To put it more plainly, whose perspective are you?

In my life I have been accused of being circular. But here, to the notion that choice implies perspective, I must add my view that a choice of perspective can lead to authenticity or its evil twin, hyperbole. A case in point is Robert Mapplethorpe. Can it really be that the significance of his photographic art resides entirely in its classical purity and beauty? I think not. One can argue that the context of his work—homosexuality, black sexuality (not its historically stereotyped opposite, bestiality), and the high society portrait—constitutes an authentic perspective on Mapplethorpe's work in addition to his aesthetics. If context drops out, is there authenticity?

Explosive issues around art inevitably place the question of authenticity in the hands of the museum director and trustees who ultimately bear responsibility for the institution. And so I come to another related view: *authenticity can be had by acknowledging different perspectives*. Consider a 1985 exhibition, "Facing History: The Black Image in American Art, 1710-1940," organized by the Corcoran Gallery of Art. During the planning stages of the project, the painful nature of its subject became increasingly clear. Here is what the curator, Guy McElroy (the late African-American art historian who died shortly after the exhibition ran in Washington, D.C., and Brooklyn), wrote in the exhibition brochure about the premise of "Facing History":

> Naming is a form of power, and visual images have the persuasive power to define place and personality. . . . Socially disastrous stereotypes, individualized and sympathetic imagery, heroic portrayals, and conflicted presentations of African Americans bear all the marks of the progress and retrenchment which characterize our national history.

It was my job to interpret the repository of black images made by American artists selected for the exhibition. It was also my job to operate mindful of the malignant confusion and guilt that disfigure debate on and literally blur our vision of the history of race in America. I decided, and both the curator and the museum leadership concurred, that "Facing History" should be just that: facing the visual history of black imagery in America. Choosing a single perspective for interpretation would have been a form of massive denial, a classic example of hyperbole regardless of the position advanced. Trying to present "all views" would have amounted to the same thing. So we convened a group with the expertise to bring McElroy's research on the art together with then-current scholarly work on the literature and documents representing the black voice in America. Charles Larson, a professor of literature at American University, Deborah Newman Ham, a specialist in African-American history and culture at the Library of Congress, and Henry (Skip) Gates, then a professor of literature at Cornell and now at Harvard, formed a panel that developed a three-tiered interpretation of the exhibition.

Our plan was pretty simple: to pair white vision and black voice. Walking through the exhibition, visitors could read wall labels explaining each object's theme. Then, beside about half of the works were labels bearing excerpts from African-American writings. Sometimes they confirmed the artist's image; sometimes they exposed it as prejudice, propaganda, or nostalgia for the "old ways." Images of blacks as buffoons, servile menials, comic entertainers, or threatening subhumans, as well as powerful and dignified portrayals were paired with writings by Countee Cullen, Langston Hughes, Paul Laurence Dunbar, Gwendolyn Brooks, and Toni Morrison. For example, the painting *Slave Market in Richmond, Virginia* (1852-53) by Eyre Crowe had two labels: one describing the painting and another bearing a passage from the first novel by an African-American author, *Clotel* (1853) by William Wells Brown. The painting label detailed the scene presented: the interior of a slave warehouse, where slaves and slave dealers wait for an auction to begin. The blacks are well dressed in long frocks and white aprons; they hold their babies on their laps. An excerpt from *Clotel* tells a different story, describing the slave auction as bestial degradation of the most intolerable kind: children torn away from mothers, adults placed on public view, chained and nude:

> This was a Southern auction, at which the bones, muscles, sinews,
>
> blood, and nerves of a young lady of sixteen were sold for five

hundred dollars; her moral character for two hundred; her improved intellect for one hundred; her Christianity for three hundred; and her chastity and virtue for four hundred dollars more. And this, too, in a city thronged with churches. . . .

The dramatic contrast between the artist's serene visual image and *Clotel*'s violent literary account accomplish the goal of acknowledging different perspectives. Each work of art—the visual and the literary—speaks with its own authority. The visitor has the power to consider the evidence.

Taken to extremes, presentation of different perspectives can result in the same "everything but the kitchen sink" nightmare that comes from too many ideas, none of them edited out. This is where the voice of objects, their artistic identity, their personal history, their materials, and the aim of their creator play an equally important role in the choice arena. What "facts" will you present to children about the French impressionist Claude Monet and one of his canvases representing Rouen Cathedral? I chose to discuss the idea of working on a subject through series painting, as Monet did with the cathedral. In the 20 versions of the subject he exhibited together in Paris in 1895 (out of a total of 30), the church's facade appears shimmery, enveloped in fog, bright, or steely depending on the individual provocations of weather and time of day Monet was trying to capture. My aim of was to encourage children to see Monet's repeated images of the same subject as not all that different from their own repetitions of pictures—the dogs and cats and imaginary figures they draw over and over, trying to "get it." I mentioned this example because artistic method is a critical aspect of art appreciation generally considered fine for adult consumption but, I think, at the same level of accuracy though in different words, really good for young learners, too. Truly, there are so many ideas about Monet from which to choose. I personally could do a whole pamphlet just on his chickens, vegetables, roots, and horticultural projects at Giverny. But I think I shall quit this while I imagine that I still have your attention and the subject is still *art*.

SOURCES

This picture, I say, seemed to consider itself the queen of the collection. It represented a woman, considerably larger, I thought, than the life. I calculated that this lady, put into a scale of magnitude suitable for the reception of a commodity of bulk, would infallibly turn from fourteen to sixteen stone. She was, indeed, extremely well fed; very much butcher's meat—to say nothing of bread, vegetables, and liquids—must she have consumed to attain that breadth and height, that wealth of muscle, that affluence of flesh. She lay half-reclined on a couch—why, it would be difficult to say; broad daylight blazed round her. She appeared in hearty health, strong enough to do the work of two plain cooks; she could not plead a weak spine; she ought to have been standing, or at least sitting bolt upright. She had no business to lounge away the noon on a sofa. She ought likewise to have worn decent garments—a gown covering her properly, which was not the case. Out of abundance of material—seven and-twenty yards, I should say, of drapery—she managed to make inefficient raiment. Then for the wretched untidiness surrounding her there could be no excuse. Pots and pans—perhaps I ought to say vases and goblets—were rolled here and there on the foreground; a perfect rubbish of flowers was mixed amongst them, and an absurd and disorderly mass of curtain upholstery smothered the couch and cumbered the floor. On referring to the catalogue, I found that this notable production bore the name *Cleopatra.*

Charlotte Brontë, *Vilette* (1853)

This passage from Brontë's last novel is a description, made by its main character Lucy Snow, of a Salon painting she comes upon while touring an art gallery. Read it slowly again, study it carefully, and you will find that it represents, as the writer David Lodge says in his book, *The Art of Fiction* (1992), an upending of art historical discourse in favor of factual recitation that exposes the "essential falsity (as the character Lucy saw it) of this kind of art."

Have you realized that Lucy was looking at a female figure of enormous size? Her clinical notice of the lady's "magnitude," estimating her weight and remarking on how "well fed" presumably with "very much butcher's meat" she had to be in order to have achieved such a remarkable "wealth of muscle" and "affluence of flesh" puts the issue of scale in a questionable rather than respectable artistic zone. She then, as we might say, deconstructs the conventions of pose and the use of drapery in "high" art. Why is the woman lying down when she should be perfectly capable of sitting up? And what's with all this yardage, Lucy asks, when the lady's still naked? Ah, Cleopatra. Are you a goddess, really?

This fabulous tear-down of a high-flying historical-mythological painting is accomplished through the literary devise called "defamiliarization," which, Lodge tells his reader, derives from the Russian word *ostranenie*—to make strange. According to Lodge, the purpose of defamiliarization is to shake off the "deadening effects of habit by representing familiar things in an unfamiliar way." You can see the advantages this strategy might have in the writing life of a museum educator. It can be a tool for digging out of the tired phrases of art history that go whizzing by a non-specialist, and replacing them with a bracing first look at the visual evidence.

I present this material to you as a way of answering the second question assigned for this essay, that is, From whom am I learning today? My sources, in addition to current scholarship in art history and methods, are in literature. At the National Gallery of Art, where I am currently head of education publications (print and electronic) for the museum's education division, my job is essentially the development of content. I also write fiction in my off hours, or at least I try to. So far, I have completed a short story that I like, a poem that scares me but it's pretty good, and a novel that is in shambles but has bite. Working on both sides of the content line, with factual material at work and imaginary material at home, I am looking more and more at the writing strategies of novelists as both learning tools and sources of ideas. I'm not saying that I work from novels, but rather that I work from their varied and innovative structures. I try, increasingly, to present information about artists, their biographies, their bodies of work, and their methods and materials in ways that will grab a reader's attention and provide vivid focus for learning. The strategy of defamiliarization is one way. And there are, as I am sure you are thinking, many others. I cannot recommend highly enough a good read of Lodge's above-mentioned book (as well as his other volumes of literary criticism and guidance) as a way of getting "fresh" with art history and aesthetics, after you have taken in all the scholarship and analysis the art experts have to offer and looked long and hard at the art itself.

Lodge's book is like a little bible. In it there are many pathways for the writing life. For example, the chapter called "Lists" shows you how certain ways of reducing what would have been discourse to a catalogue of (carefully chosen) items can train intense light on an important cache of interests or issues in an artist's work. In "Introducing a Character," Lodge explains how the description of an individual basically uses a technique called synecdoche, in which "the part [stands] for the whole." What does that mean to me? It's choice, again. As Lodge points out, it is the act of being "highly selective" about the facts you present that can bring a person into high relief. And that is what I strive for when I put together information about artists and works of art. Think about Paul Cézanne and his images of the Château Noir, an unfinished, abandoned house located in dense, rocky woods on the outskirts of the artist's hometown, Aix-en-Provence. You could write forever about Cézanne's birthplace and his life. But of the points that will powerfully relate his "living" to the images of the house, I have chosen: "Cézanne knew the region of Aix intimately; he had walked it and painted it throughout his life. In his later years, he sought out the isolated locations around Aix, where the land was more rugged, remote, and perhaps indicative of his own moodiness."

Time-shift. Surprise. Repetition. They are also among Lodge's fascinating chapters, all of which enrich my approach to art historical materials I need to absorb, organize, and synthesize for vividness, utility, and inspiration. I leave you with a wish that literature will also aid you in seeing the life and work of art through the lens of creativity provided by our great writers. At the moment I am re-reading *Lolita*, whose author, Vladimir Nabokov, in my view, is one of the great-est writers of all time. In addition to his rank as a master of prose, Nabokov was an expert on butterflies and traveled across the country on butterfly collection trips. Those expeditions were the source of Humbert Humbert's car trip across America with his adolescent protegée, Dolores, Dolly, Lo, Lo-lee-ta. Read it again, and you will find in both the text and the postscript a gold mine of inspiration for your work in museum education.

IS THERE METHOD IN OUR MADNESS? IMPROVISATION IN THE PRACTICE OF MUSEUM EDUCATION

by Mary Ellen Munley

What is the role of museum education? What kinds of programs and activities should be part of museum education departments? Is there a coherent vision behind the expansion of museum education beyond structuring and guiding field trips to promoting a variety of learning activities—after-school programs, literacy programs, festivals, speaker series, symposia, overnight events, summer camps, library collaborations, programs for parents, video productions, Web sites, interactive exhibits, museum schools, and electronic field trips? What are we to make of this seemingly endless variety of offerings? Have we gone mad?

One of the challenges museum educators face is to ensure that there is a guiding vision for program development so that museums are presenting something more than a hodge-podge collection of public activities. To understand the essential vision and value of museum education, it is instructive to reflect on the improvisational quality of many recent educational programs. For a successful educator is one who responds to changing times by improvising new programs while remaining focused on the underlying convictions that provide continuity and direction. Variation has allowed museums to evolve, but constancy has set our course.

In her remarkable book, *Composing a Life*, author Mary Catherine Bateson recommends using the forms and practice of improvisational jazz to understand growth, development, and change. Bateson's writings on women's lives have influenced my own thoughts on museum education. She offers a framework for understanding accomplishment when the path is not a traditional one: "Each of us has worked by improvisation, discovering the shape of our creation along the way, rather than pursuing a vision already defined . . . solving problems for the first time . . . [finding it] no longer possible to follow the paths of previous generations."[1]

Indeed, museum educators work by experimentation. They must be responsive to the public, and they are often the first to identify the barriers that keep people away from museums and their collections. Museum educators identify problems, turn them into challenges, and improvise responses. Their improvisation has resulted in many "firsts" for museums, including outreach programs, neighborhood museums, discovery rooms, gallery games, interactive exhibits, community advisory groups, and museum schools. These programs may not have been anticipated, but they were carefully crafted nonetheless.

There is, I believe, a pattern underlying the variations. Together, these solo improvisations create an evolving definition of museums as educational institutions. As Bateson writes, "Practicing improvisation [is] clearly not a contradiction. Jazz exemplifies artistic activity that is at once individual and communal, performance that is both repetitive and innovative, each participant sometimes providing background support and sometimes flying free."[2]

This collective act of creativity is at the heart of museum education. Despite all the variation and improvisation, there are underlying convictions that provide continuity and direction to this work. As Bateson writes, "Improvisation can be either a last resort or an established way of evoking creativity."[3] I believe that the improvisational art of responding to new situations with focused innovations has allowed museum education to evolve and has strengthened the educational relevance of museums in modern times. This has happened—and will continue to happen—because there are some fundamental principles that guide the practice of museum education. If we remain true to these convictions, we will lose neither our minds nor our way as we delve into the limitless possibilities of program format and design.

THE FOUNDATIONS OF MUSEUM EDUCATION

Our work as museum educators is predicated on our beliefs about our audiences and our beliefs about human learning and capacity for understanding. It is these beliefs that set the foundation for our evolving vision for the museum experience.

What do we believe about our audiences? In many museums, there is a decided tension between audiences and professional staff, and that tension can be traced to very different ideas about what a museum is and why people visit. Most people do not go to museums with the intention of being students who will learn what the teacher (the museum) has decided they should know. Yet museum staff, who have planned each detail of an exhibit or program, frequently become frustrated, even angry, with visitors who "fail" to follow their lead, go in the "right" direction, or attend sufficiently to the intended message.

At issue here is something very fundamental: the ability to understand who our visitors are and what coming to the museum means to them. Traveling, rather than schooling, strikes me as a useful metaphor for understanding museum-going. With leisure travel, experience accumulates over time. Travel can be fun, not tedious. We are attentive to our own needs when we travel. When visiting a new place, we do not feel the obligation to focus only on history, geography, architecture, and "high" culture. We allow ourselves to explore the landscape in a holistic way. We concern ourselves with the comforts of accommodations. We soak in the ambiance. We can delight in the cuisine without being considered frivolous. The point is that we bring our entire person—mind, heart, body—when we travel. Rarely are we invited to bring so much of ourselves to a place of learning—to a museum. But if museums create an atmosphere in which their visitors can think, feel, and sense, they will begin to better understand their audiences, and rethink the design of their exhibits, programs, food services, rest areas, and more.

Coming to terms with visitors' needs and interests is at the heart of attempts to expand and diversify audiences—a hallmark of museum education activities for decades. Although demographic profiles of visitors to most museums do not support our claims, most museum professionals believe that museums are for everyone.

We need to understand the ramifications of our commitment to broaden and expand our audiences. To accomplish this goal, we will work with and serve people from diverse racial and ethnic backgrounds, people who have not been part of the museum world in the past. We will serve the very young and the very old, and we will serve people who draw a wide range of meanings from the museum experience. As we invite more people to visit museums and actively participate in many different ways, we may wonder if our programming is still educational. Obviously, the answer to this question depends on how we define education.

What do we believe about education and the capacity for human beings to learn? At its best, museum learning encourages independent thought. Museums have the capacity to stimulate meaningful learning for their visitors. Meaningful learning is about making connections, and it occurs when new information is linked with existing concepts in the visitor's system of understanding. Meaningful learning results in visitors creating a variety of messages and meanings.

Therefore, many museum educators do not expect, or even aim, for each visitor to learn the same thing. Each visitor will experience the museum differently because there are endless and unpredictable ways in which people acquire, retain, and use knowledge. In fact, it is this unpredictability—indeed, the creative imagination—that is at the heart of the educational matter in museums.

Research in the fields of human learning, cognition and human intelligence suggests radical shifts in how we design exhibits, programs, and learning experiences. Most widely touted, certainly in the museum world, is the work of Howard Gardner. Identifying musical, spatial, bodily kinesthetic, interpersonal and intrapersonal intelligences along with the verbal and logical mathematical intelligences, he places many people among the ranks of talented human beings for the first time. He thereby challenges educational institutions of all types to rethink their aims and their designs. For museums, this rethinking challenges us to expand the traditional role of the museum as educator.

THE FUTURE OF MUSEUM EDUCATION

These two beliefs structure the evolution of educational programming as museum educators strive to provoke independent thought and foster active participation in museum programs by a broader audience. Museums therefore offer a range of learning experiences. Some engage our visitors with the traditional program formats that will continue to be valuable in sharing what we know. However, the traditional way of thinking about museum education offerings (i.e., workshops, classes for schools, and family programs) is simply not robust enough to address the needs of an expanded audience and an expanded definition of human learning. Although lists of program ideas come easily, more of the same is not an advisable direction for most museum education departments. We must break with tradition and develop new approaches to program development and design that reflect our expanded audiences and an expanded understanding of learning. To do this, we must establish the museum as a center of learning in the community. The following presents one possible framework for understanding how museum education is evolving.

1. The museum as educator. Museum programs have the capacity to inform people of all ages. Content knowledge is important, and museums will continue to excel in introducing large public audiences to valuable information about art, science, history, and more. Education programs focused on sharing information are important first steps in educating our audiences.

In addition to information exchange, museums have the potential to address important societal issues. Through a mixture of entertaining, inspiring, enlightening, and challenging experiences, museum programs can inform people of all ages about science, technology, history, the environment, and cultural diversity. However, education is not just sharing what we know. It is also about encouraging conversation and participation. Museum educators should respond creatively to this challenge by developing programming innovations that will allow institutions to remain meaningful and purposeful by evolving into community centers, community forums, and community catalysts.

2. The museum as public forum. Museum programs can introduce participants to thoughtful presentations and discussions about complex and important global, national, and community issues. Working in partnership with community leaders and organizations, museums can give life to their mission and collections by organizing meetings, lectures, and debates on topics important to our collective quality of life. In their capacity as forums, museums also can invite people to meet on site and use collections and exhibits as stimuli for reflection and discussion.

3. The museum as community center. Museums create community spaces. They have the capacity to unite people who would not normally meet. If we create inviting spaces and more open-ended programs, over time people of all backgrounds will come together to share social learning experiences. Indeed, museums have a history of fashioning programs around drumming, storytelling, dancing, cooking, and festivals—forms and formats used through the ages by people with an interest in coming together. The new twist for museums and their audiences is that these programs can be ongoing and the participants can be performers, not observers. Museums can, for instance, establish storytelling and drumming circles, dance groups, artist colonies, and ecology groups.

4. The museum as provocateur. Why do humans fight change? How is technology changing our world? Why do we see hate crimes in our communities? How can we sustain the biodiversity the planet needs? What will we do about the fact that so many children do not know how to read? Museums need not steer completely clear of today's complex and difficult social issues. In fact, if they do, it will be to their peril. Through exhibits, programs, and community partnerships, museums can provoke discussion and actively participate in projects that strive to achieve goals related to literacy, cultural understanding, and sustaining our natural environment.

5. The museum as catalyst. To the extent that our programs are successful, others will build on them. As museums emerge as vital community learning centers, they will be among the institutions setting the agenda for their communities.

The museum as educator. The museum as forum. The museum as community center. The museum as provocateur. The museum as catalyst. To some, this vision for expanding the role of the museum may seem too far afield, too ambitious, too insane. However, to borrow another insight, "Though this be madness, yet there is method in't."[4] If we stay true to our convictions about our audiences and learning, our course is set. Through our creative and purposeful improvisation, it will be achieved.

I would like to thank Jennifer Eagleton for her invaluable assistance in preparing this essay.

REFERENCES

1. Mary Catherine Bateson, *Composing a Life* (New York: Penguin Books, 1991), pp. 1-2.

2. Ibid., pp. 2-3.

3. Ibid., p. 4.

4. William Shakespeare, *Hamlet*, act 2, sc. 2, line 222.

ELEGANT PROGRAMS
AND CONVERSATIONS

by Michael Spock

As a practitioner working in the public side of museums, I am always fascinated by the sharp distinction between encounters with museum objects and exhibits on the one hand, and staff-led programs and conversations among staff and visitors on the other. These programmatic and conversational exchanges that we orchestrate or facilitate seem very different from the experiences we try to provoke with objects and exhibits: one is highly personal and social, the other quite arms-length and impersonal. Although I have been drawn to and spent more time working with and thinking about objects and exhibits, I would like to claim this educator-sponsored moment to explore some of the things that surround the social and personal side of this interpretive equation—narrative museum programming and informal museum conversations—and then speculate about what these human qualities do for us in contrast with relatively impersonal museum objects and exhibits.

A few years ago, as an exploratory exercise to get us started looking at the nature of learning in museums, Deborah Perry, Hope Jensen Leichter, John Paterson, and I set up videotaping equipment at the Association of Youth Museums and American Association of Museums conferences in Philadelphia and asked you, our colleagues, to tell us stories about pivotal learning experiences in museums. In our 76 interviews, we collected hundreds of fascinating stories.

As we immersed ourselves in these personal and professional memories, I was struck by how neatly your stories paralleled and resonated with my own museum experiences. So I would like to take a look at a few of those vivid moments—yours and mine—and see if we can figure out why they seemed pivotal to us and worth sharing, and what they can tell us about this more frankly personal and social side of museum-going.

Let's begin this reflective exercise with two stories firmly rooted in the tradition of narrative interpretation—programming that tells a story. First, a story from my museum going, and then a story from one of our colleagues. As you read them, think about how they differ from interactions with objects and exhibits.

At Old Sturbridge Village, a taciturn blacksmith pulls at his overhead bellows, and we stand our ground against the intimidating wave of heat that washes across our faces. He extracts a slender, bright-tipped bar of metal from the coals and begins to shape it on his anvil: tapping it, turning it, working it, slowly, carefully, into a long, tapered point. Pausing, the blacksmith lays the now dark-red tip crosswise on an upside-down chisel set into a hole in his anvil. Three inches of pointed bar hang out beyond the chisel's edge. He begins to beat on the metal just above the chisel, slowly turning it with his gloved left hand until the bar is nearly cut through. The tip hangs by an iron thread. The smith stops, grabs a pair of hand-wrought pliers from a careless pile of grimy tools, and twists off the tip. Too bad, he's made a mistake. He's going to have to throw it away and start over. But instead he shoves the tip, point first, into a small square hole punched in a thick metal plate. Turning the plate over, he lays it on the anvil with the point sticking down below, alongside the anvil, and pounds the quarter-inch remnant of the cut bar sticking above the plate. The nub begins to mushroom out and—suddenly getting it—we exclaim in unison, "It's a nail!"

I returned to this experience, years later, in trying to grasp the improbable pre-industrial economics of burning old houses to the ground to salvage their precious hand-made nails.

In this excerpt from our collection of your memories, Randee Humphrey, director of education at the Richmond Children's Museum, Va., tells a similar story—about a story. Our second example of narrative interpretation is a classically structured, although extraordinarily inventive, visitor program.

I was new to the community, and I was searching out opportunities for my son. He was three and a half at the time. And I read of a story time at the Children's Museum. . . . And upon arriving at the Children's Museum, encountered a very wonderful gentleman (who was there with his child in tow), who was the storyteller for the day. It was not in the traditional sense of story hour—reading a story—but actually telling or guiding a story. Assembled in the room were mothers and some fathers, but mostly mothers, with small children about the same age as my son. And we all gathered around and after just a few brief introductions, this man began leading a story about going fishing.

So we were all part of this imaginary fishing trip. And we gathered all our gear together, and we talked about the fishing rods and where the bait comes from and what other equipment we were going to need. And we talked about where we would go to fish. And then we went to the place where we [were] fishing through an imaginary trip that we all took together. And then we arrived at the fishing spot and all went through the process of . . . bait[ing] our hooks, casting out our line, reeling in our fish. And it was a wonderful engaging time for the children and the parents as we all proceeded to cast out and reel in and look at what we had caught.

The pivotal moment for me though was when this man then congratulated us all on having caught our fish and opened up an ice chest, [in which] he had brought fish to the museum that morning. And these were fish fully intact, with their heads and their tails and the scales and everything. . . . And all of us gathered around as he proceeded to clean them and to bone them and to filet them and to show the children all the various parts of the fish that we had just caught in our imaginations. And then he also hooked up a little frying pan and put in the cooking oil and fileted these fish and cut them into small pieces and breaded them and proceeded to fry these little chunks of fish, which we then, a few minutes later, had the opportunity to all sample. And when I left that day, I mean it was—it was an incredible experience. . . . Having this moment of sharing and then having it culminate in this moment that engaged so many other senses.

Our other category of personalized and socialized interpretation is the informal conversations that spring up, spontaneously or with a little prompting, between staff and visitors, or among visitors themselves. Again, as you read these stories think about what makes them different from interpretive experiences you have had with objects and exhibits.

This story, about a visitor-led exchange, was told by my friend, the late Steve Borysewicz, former exhibit developer at the Field Museum of Natural History. The usual roles of interpreter-learner appear to have been reversed.

In eighth grade, my mom was teaching school. She said, "There's this really cool kid in one of my classes." Because I liked going and looking at art when I was little a lot. And he was in fourth grade. She said, "Why don't you go to the Art Institute with him, because he's never been?" He was a little, inner-city kid, and we all grew up in the inner city. So, I went with him and it was like the first time that I'd ever gone on like, what amounted to a teaching trip with somebody younger than me. I was used to being the little kid and having adults, older cousins, tell me stuff.

And it was really fun to go with him and listen to what he had to say about pictures.

We looked at this David portrait. And David's a really interesting painter because he's a very realistic painter. And it's appealing to kids because he had this intense sense of detail. This painting of a woman that he'd done that was just intricate. Her clothing was perfect. You could make out all her facial features. The light was really even, like portrait lighting. And she's sewing, but she's not holding a needle or thread. And yet, her hands are in this sewing position.

And this kid I was with just went off on that completely. He could not get over how much she looked so much like she was doing something but was holding nothing. He just talked and talked about what that meant, and why did she want her picture painted that way? And, why did he do it that way? And, why didn't she just have her hands in her lap? Or, why didn't he put the needle in her hand? And maybe she was trying to—and he had this whole, long idea about maybe she was trying to show that she had something useful to do, even though it was obvious that she was a rich lady. And I mean, that was his reading on it. It was really cool.

And then, he started doing that to all these other pictures that we would come to. And he felt like that's what he was supposed to be doing and that it was fun. And it was really fun. You know, to talk to him about it and just make up stories and kind of think about it.

From my own repertoire of museum memories this final story surfaced. Plimoth Plantation staffs its realistically scruffy reconstructed village with costumed interpreters trained to go about their homely chores without stepping out of character and context.

We wander into one of the thatched homes where the mistress of the house is poking up the fire. She pulls a shawl more tightly around her shoulders against the damp and lifts a pot of stew off the fireplace crane and sets it and two wooden bowls on the table. The mistress is joined at the table by a tired-looking man, the family's indentured servant. They sit down to eat, and while we lean in, looking over their shoulders, they tuck the stew away, unselfconsciously using their fingers. The conversation turns to the thinness of the harvest. They agree that the coming winter, like the last two, will be hard. The cold and disease are bad enough, but their real concern is that they have not been able to put up enough food and fodder to see them through.

When the table is cleared, I ask the mistress how they keep warm through the challenging New England winters. She says that it is almost impossible, that she suffers from chilblains, but considers herself blessed as several members of the community died during the last two winters. But the animals suffer more since their feed runs low by spring. It will be important to slaughter some pigs and sheep soon to conserve their fodder.

She asks if things have been as bad where we come from. I have to confess that winter can be unpleasant, but not that challenging since we have a furnace to keep us warm, go to a supermarket to restock our larder, and only have a dog and cat to care for. The mistress is puzzled and curious. What is this "furnace?" Isn't that what is used to make iron? And how could there be a market? There can't be enough people or surplus food and goods to warrant starting a market in this God-forsaken wilderness. And how can we manage without livestock?

We continue this probing dialogue: I try to appreciate the extreme limitations of her existence while she cannot begin to fathom the unimaginable technologies of my 20th-century, postindustrial life. It's hard work for us both, explaining and exploring every assumption that underlies our daily lives and how much we take for granted.

So what are the unifying themes among this rich material? Why did our colleagues and I decide to tell these particular stories as examples of pivotal museum learning experiences? What was it about these programs and conversations that stood out? That made them different from equally wonderful experiences we have had with exhibits and objects?

My first observation springs from a defining quality of these encounters: they are mediated by people—live people. In contrast to the impersonal, fixed exhibit medium, programs and conversations derive their strength, flexibility, and connectedness from being human exercises. Each of these stories acknowledges and celebrates this special quality.

Humans are social animals who generally, though not always, come alive in the presence of other people. Good museum programmers and engaged visitors surf on this social need using it to bridge objects to ideas to people. As much as we can be turned on by wonderful objects and informed by splendid exhibits, they don't exploit this human quality and, therefore, do not do their work in the same way, nor cover the same intellectual territory. This is not meant to deny the fact that for shy people impersonal displays can be a relief, or that many of us will do anything we can to avoid being kidnapped by the house tour guide. Yet most of us, most of the time, are nourished by the personal exchanges afforded by visitor programs and conversations with our companions.

These experiences are interactive. Rather than being passive receptacles, the visitor contributes to, constructs, helps creates the experience. The thoughtful programmer and companion always elicit this involvement. The fishers are asked to imagine baiting their hooks. The mistress of the house insists that I explain the circumstances of my life. Steve and his charge wrestle with why David did what he did with the woman's hand. By not saying anything and just letting the process unfold, even the blacksmith keeps us speculating until the very end about what he might be making. Current learning theory posits that all memories are constructed by the learner when the content of the program/lesson/message is worked against and within the interior context of the learner's past experiences.

These programs have a conversational flavor—even if no words are spoken. These conversations have a content focus—even if they are not part of an obvious lesson. There is an assumption the visitor or companion is not some poor soul in need of enlightenment, but a smart and capable collaborator. So it isn't just that visitors are expected to work for their insights, but that they might actually have something interesting to contribute to the exchange. The conversations at Plimoth and Chicago, the programs at Richmond and Sturbridge all imply mutual respect and nicely balanced investments.

Unlike the fixed exhibit medium, good live programming and conversations are flexible and adaptable. When the visitor is not being engaged, the programmer or companion can shift gears, try something else, punt. Even in the heavily scripted program, and in contrast to the more drawn-out and sometimes irrevocable exhibit development process, good programs and conversations are adjusted from moment to moment in real time. This is especially evident in exchanges with individuals and small groups, where we can be responsive to specific and evolving interests and needs. The mistress of the house can ask me to take her down an unexplored road. The boy's discovery of the needle-less hand can be the take-off for a shared adventure.

Another contrast to exhibits is that these programs are better at illuminating processes and telling stories: things that change, that have a beginning, middle, and an end. Even the most structured exhibit cannot count on the sequential attention of the visitor. When cornered by the demands of serial content, exhibitors fall back on fiber-optic displays, motor-driven models, audiovisual shows. The fishing story and nail making have this quality of beautifully paced, tightly sequenced events: nothing is out of place, nothing happens before its time, nothing is superfluous.

Despite the many channels that we have developed for animating the exhibit experience, our repertoire of sensual options still seems richer in the visitor program and casual conversation. Fish can be smelled and tasted, the heat of the forge and ring of the anvil felt, the grime under the fingers of the plantation interpreter directly observed. Here, words, pictures, real things—no matter how eloquent—don't convey the same information to the same people in the same way. Howard Gardner's multiple intelligences require playing to multiple senses.

Finally, the object/exhibit versus program/conversation distinction might best be expressed with a term I learned from my physicist and mathematician friends: these stories all illustrated elegantly orchestrated or improvised events. They were so focused on the main idea; so stripped of extraneous clutter; so open to the peculiar needs and contributions of the content and participant; and they so beautifully bridged content to audience with just the right medium of exchange that it seemed in retrospect that they could not have happened in any other way. None could have been good exhibits. Each in this sense was an elegant solution to its respective educational or social challenge.

I think what we storytellers may be saying is that the social/personal equation counts for a lot among our museum memories. Even the taciturn blacksmith's craftsmanship draws us, like the iron he works, into the quality and pace of his very human life and, without saying a word, expresses the value to the community of his labors and skills. And whether we are talking about these sorts of exquisitely structured programs or more spontaneous exchanges, our stories all celebrate the contributions we humans—alive and engaged—can make to explorations of the objective world and wonderful things.

This research was supported by contributions from the Joyce Foundation, the James L. and John S. Knight Foundation, Children's Museums: Bridges to the Future, the Arts Management Program, Mandel Center for Non-Profit Organizations, Case Western Reserve University, and the Chapin Hall Center for Children.

REAL PEARLS AT THE POSTMODERN MUSEUM POTLUCK: CONSTRUCTIVISM AND INCLUSIVENESS

by Marlene Chambers

urprising as it may seem to many readers of "The Importance of Being Élitist," Calvin Tomkins's *New Yorker* profile of Metropolitan Museum of Art director Philippe de Montebello (Nov. 24, 1997), it was not Thomas Hoving who first brought bread and circuses to the museum table. A populist stance and the concept of rational entertainment have both been part and parcel of the educational mission of American museums for more than 200 years. From the outset, these institutions saw themselves as important cogs in a society founded on democratic ideals—as schools for the enlightenment and moral improvement of the common man. But, like Charles Willson Peale, who was the first among them to admit that museums must "amuse as well as instruct," early museum proprietors depended entirely on admission fees for survival, and they ignored Peale's axiom at their peril.[1] The dialectic between the competing poles of scholarship and popularization, research and education, elitism and inclusiveness colors the whole course of museum history in America. And, for at least the last century, the very meaning of education has been a bone of political, theoretical, and practical contention within the profession. No one has argued against the idea that museums should teach visitors about the collections, but exactly who, what, why, and how they should teach have constantly been at issue.

Early on in these controversies, George Brown Goode, assistant secretary of the Smithsonian Institution, managed to voice elitist and populist views simultaneously in an influential indictment delivered to the American Historical Association in 1888. In almost the same breath, he espoused the opposing views held by the Smithsonian's first two secretaries, Joseph Henry and Spencer Baird: he attacked early museums for dumbing down to attract a public interested only in entertainment and deplored the exclusiveness of those that catered solely to the interests of scholars and intellectuals.[2] Fifty years later, not long after museums began to add educators to their staffs, Francis Henry Taylor, then director of the same Met whose current director believes that elitism "is the very essence of democracy, in that it seeks to bring as many people as possible to a higher level of understanding and appreciation,"[3] castigated museums for concocting a diet too rich for the common man: "And since education has been defined as 'the art of casting artificial pearls before real swine,' it is only natural that museum workers should have concerned themselves with the elaborate furnishing of the trough at the expense of the digestive capacity of the feeders."[4]

The controversy continues today at the highest administrative and most basic philosophical levels although it has been almost a century since educators entered the museum work force and 25 years since the Standing Professional Committee on Museum Education was founded as the first such special interest committee under the aegis of the American Association of Museums (AAM). In her recently published *From Knowledge to Narrative: Educators and the Changing Museum*, Lisa C. Roberts credits educators with effecting a transformation of the institution in the past two and a half decades and claims that their success in "bringing other voices and views to the museum floor" has led to a questioning of traditional assumptions about both authority and the nature of knowledge. She sees today's movement toward the inclusion of visitors in the interpretive process, especially as articulated in the *Excellence and Equity* report adopted by the AAM Board of Directors in May 1991,[5] as evidence of a shift that has been taking place from the definition of education as an authoritative (and authoritarian) ladling out of immutable knowledge toward the idea that education is a "meaning making" activity requiring cooperative negotiation between visitors and institution.[6] I agree with her optimistic view that great strides have been made in this direction and that we stand now at a moment of unsurpassed opportunity, but I am not confident that we have seen the end of the old elitist concept of education as a *noblesse oblige* activity in which the haves dish out pearls of wisdom to the have-nots. Nor am I convinced that many professional museum educators even know about, much less embrace and practice, the constructivist theory of education as "narrative endeavor" that Roberts explicates with such clarity and grace.[7]

As Roberts points out, there are two key differences between the traditional model of education in which knowledge can only flow downhill from teacher to learner and the constructivist model that invites the learner to observe, compare, and evaluate the stories we tell ourselves to make sense of the world. The constructivist model is, first of all, more inclusive, more respectful of the world view visitors bring with them to the museum. Whereas the didactic model is grounded in the belief that knowledge exists independently of both teacher and learner, the constructivist model sees knowledge as an intellectual construct subject to constant review and revision. By explicitly admitting that the narrative construction it presents is only one of a number of possible versions, the constructivist model, as Roberts says, actually "frees museums to take a stand and be explicit in their expression of issues in which they have a vested interest."[8]

The other difference between the constructivist model and the traditional model is that the constructivist model allows for shared authority in meaning making. By admitting there is room for disagreement, ambiguity, complexity, and other perspectives, it actively encourages visitors to compare and evaluate the museum's perspective against their own and others. Critical thinking is an inherent part of the constructivist model.

But it is exactly these differences that make the constructivist theory of education threatening to those who are used to taking their role as truth-givers for granted. For many, the admission that there are other possible ways of interpreting the world and the things in it implies a devaluation of their own perspective and seems to let loose a kind of anarchy in which anything goes. It may even first appear that there is no role for education in a system that recognizes the plausibility of multiple visions of the world. Yet, as Roberts explains, it is the task of education to facilitate experiences in which world visions can collide and re-form through the process of observing, comparing, and assessing their relative value in various contexts.[9] For it is only when experience challenges our expectations that we stop to examine our currently held intellectual construct about the world and, building on past meanings, create a new world of meaning. I think it is still doubtful whether museum educators (and other museum workers) will want to give up the sense of control that comes from taking what Jerome Bruner calls the "paradigmatic" or "logico-scientific" approach in order to adopt what he refers to as the "narrative" or storytelling approach of constructivist philosophy.[10] The shift is fraught with difficulties and presents a challenge to some of the most dearly held values of a profession that has historically focused on transmitting content, not process. Sharing authority can be scary, and uncertain outcomes still make many uncomfortable, even in an age in which science itself has accepted the uncertainty principle.

Nonetheless, there are encouraging signs of change. The framers of *Excellence and Equity*, for instance, include exploration, critical thinking, and dialogue as components of their broad definition of education.[11] Yet, how many consciously devised opportunities for meaningful dialogue can actually be found in today's museum exhibitions? How often do exhibit elements invite the sort of exploration and critical thinking essential to the process of finding meaning in objects? How many gallery devices actually coach visitors in the use of skills? Instead, we still usually find the soporific model of the textbook and lecture hall driving the educational components of museum exhibits. And though many museum educators have done their best to make traditional information-driven labels more user friendly by making them shorter, livelier, and less complex, the net result of their efforts has been to effect cosmetic, "literary" changes rather than to explore revolutionary educational strategies.[12] It is discouraging to find that Roberts has to go back to a label I myself developed almost a decade ago when she is casting about for examples of practical strategies for inspiring visitors to discover and construct their own narratives.[13]

Two recent exhibitions designed to encourage exploration, critical thinking, and dialogue leaped to mind when I began searching for signs of increasing acceptance of the view that museum education is a narrative endeavor.[14] Curator Robert Cohon credits his experiences teaching Art 101 at the University of Missouri-Kansas City with shaping many of the educational techniques incorporated in "Discovery and Deceit: Archaeology and the Forger's Craft" at the Nelson-Atkins Museum of Art.[15] Cohon tells how he learned the hard way that his students became overwhelmed if he tried to teach them everything he had learned through years of study. Instead, he found that a question-and-answer format could energize a roomful of students who were nodding off during lectures. By focusing the "Discovery and Deceit" exhibition on a limited number of themes and objects and by making the viewer "an active participant in the quest for knowing [which objects were] forged and what was genuine," Cohon and his team hoped, he says, to inspire dialogue.[16] And, according to indexes recently developed by Beverly Serrell, the exhibition did succeed in engaging visitors' interest. It ranked among the most "thoroughly used" in a database collected since 1993 at more than 100 exhibitions in museums of all types.[17]

The second example, "Fashion Pathways: American Indian Wearable Art," has not opened at the Denver Art Museum (DAM) at the time I write, and it will not be as overtly interactive as the Kansas City exhibition. It does, however, go much further in encouraging visitors to construct narratives about what they see and to compare their own with other, equally plausible narratives. The idea for the exhibition grew out of the live "Indian Style Show" DAM curator Frederic Douglas developed in 1942 as part of his nationwide campaign to lift Indian art out of the category of ethnography and into the realm of art.[18] Over the next 13 years, Douglas emceed more than 200 shows before almost 300,000 people from Seattle to Miami and Boston to San Diego. The exhibition will include excerpts from Douglas's scripts (for which he prepared by poring over copies of *Vogue* to learn the jargon of fashion) and period photos and news clippings, as well as comments by American Indian women of today—all specifically linked to about 30 dresses used in Douglas's shows that will be rotated during the 10-month run of the exhibition. The two curators of "Fashion Pathways," DAM's Nancy Blomberg and Nancy Parezo, curator of ethnology at Arizona State Museum, have planned an exhibition that will juxtapose multiple narratives about the clothing on view—Douglas's laudable (but, in today's climate, somewhat naive) narrative that aims to break down negative stereotypes about American Indians by showing the "common love of all women for beautiful clothes" (itself a stereotype that will not be lost on viewers) and the narratives of a number of different contemporary American Indian women.[19]

Whether the exhibition's creators will be quite as up-front as Roberts would like about their own process of narrative construction and whether they will send an explicit message that the knowledge they present is "derived through a never-ending process of discovery and revision . . . subject to ongoing debate" remains to be seen.[20] It is clear, however, that the exhibition will carry the implicit message that the meaning and value of objects is not innate, but subject to multiple interpretations over time and across cultures.

It may be significant that the idea for these exhibitions originated with curators, not educators. Certainly, curators' growing awareness of the needs and expectations of the museum visitor supports Roberts's view that educators have transformed the museum. These signs of the educator's success as an audience advocate bode well for *Excellence and Equity*'s call to make education central to the museum's mission. But there are still few indications that museums have actually begun to understand education as a meaning-making process and to value objects for their power to evoke personal narrative constructs. Inclusiveness is, as Roberts says, "one of the great buzzwords of our day." It remains to be seen whether museums will rise to the challenge of finding ways to include visitors as full partners in meaning making. Are we really ready for a potluck?

REFERENCES

1. Charles Willson Peale, quoted in Lisa C. Roberts, *From Knowledge to Narrative: Educators and the Changing Museum* (Washington and London: Smithsonian Institution Press, 1997), p. 24. Roberts's brilliant analysis of the evolution of educational theory and practice in museums has no peer in the professional literature. I am deeply indebted to her for opening new avenues of thought to me.

2. "Museum-History and Museums of History," *Papers of the American Historical Association*, ed. Herbert Baxter Adams (New York: G. P. Putnam's Sons, 1888), 3: 497-520, quoted in Roberts, p. 22.

3. Philippe de Montebello, quoted in Calvin Tomkins, "The Importance of Being Élitist," *New Yorker*, Nov. 24, 1997, p. 62.

4. Francis Henry Taylor, "Museums in a Changing World" (paper delivered at the American Association of Museums meeting, San Francisco, June 26, 1939), printed in *Atlantic Monthly* 164, no. 6 (1939): 785-92, and quoted in Roberts, p. 162, n. 16.

5. "Each visitor supplies yet another context and another layer of meaning by bringing individual experiences and values to the encounter with objects in a museum setting." From *Excellence and Equity: Education and the Public Dimension of Museums* (Washington, D.C.: American Association of Museums, 1992), p. 12.

6. Roberts's last chapter, "Education as Narrative Endeavor" (pp. 131-52), describes the "rather different animal" into which museum education appears to be evolving. In it, she speculates about the profession's future direction based on the debatable assumption that most museum workers have accepted the premise that "education is not just about museums teaching visitors; it is about visitors using museums in ways that are personally significant to them." This shift seems to Roberts to mean that the time is ripe for the adoption of the constructivist theory of education, which distinguishes between scientific and narrative modes of knowing as expounded by philosopher Nelson Goodman (*Of Mind and Other Matters* [Cambridge, Mass.: Harvard University Press, 1984]); psychologist Jerome Bruner (*Actual Minds, Possible Worlds* [Cambridge, Mass.: Harvard University Press, 1986]), and philosopher Jean-François Lyotard (*The Postmodern Condition: A Report on Knowledge*, trans. Geoff Bennington and Brian Massumi [Minneapolis: University of Minnesota Press, 1984]). Goodman's "constructivist" philosophy, which he refers to as a "philosophy of understanding," has provided the basis and name for a theory that views education as the activity of making and remaking the world when experience contradicts expectations based on prior understanding. The application of this theory to the informal learning setting of the museum certainly seems particularly apt and appears to hold great promise.

7. Museum consultant Daryl Fischer has drawn my attention to an Internet discussion on constructivism that took place through Museum-L in June 1997 among curators and educators from different types of museums. Although the exchange was lively and (generally) enthusiastic about what's happening today in the "museum-ed biz," only one of the perhaps dozen participants seemed to have a glimmer about what constructivist theory meant or how it might work in practice. Describing a year-long project at the Naturalist Center of the National Museum of Natural History, Smithsonian Institution, Richard Efthim explained how the constructivist model had been used to help nine teachers find ways to integrate museum resources and constructivist teaching strategies into their classrooms. He writes that the teachers had to "construct" for themselves in order to understand what constructivism was: "We asked them lots of questions to help them think problems through, we brainstormed lots of ideas together, and, by meeting biweekly through the year, gave them constant reinforcement and opportunities for dialogue."

8. Roberts, p. 145.

9. Roberts, p. 133.

10. Bruner, p. 11.

11. *Excellence and Equity*, p. 6. Though these are worthy, and even possibly open-ended, non-authoritarian educational goals and methods, they do not necessarily depend on a knowledge or acceptance of constructivist thinking.

12. Beverly Serrell's recent *Exhibit Labels: An Interpretive Approach* (Walnut Creek, Calif.; London; and New Delhi: AltaMira Press, 1996) provides an excellent practical guide to user-friendly label writing that is fully integrated into exhibition goals.

13. Roberts, p. 144. This experimental label (first published in "To Create Discovery," *Museum News*, May/June 1989, pp. 41-44; described by Roberts, p. 71; prototype illus. in Serrell, p. 93) was based primarily on psychologist Mihaly Csikszentmihalyi's flow-experience model (*Beyond Boredom and Anxiety* [San Francisco: Jossey-Bass Publishers, 1975]). Guided by the views Csikszentmihalyi expresses in "Human Behavior and the Science Center" (*Science Learning in the Informal Setting*, Paul G. Heltne and Linda A. Marquardt, eds. [Chicago: The Chicago Academy of Sciences, 1988], pp. 79-87), I have since argued for even less rigidly controlled discovery experiences ("Beyond 'Aha!': Motivating Museum Visitors," *ASTC Newsletter*, July/August 1989, pp. 5 and 8). There can be little doubt that Csikszentmihalyi's work on "flow" has significant implications for anyone interested in developing practical strategies for implementing constructivist theory.

Aside from my "If you like/If you don't like this painting" label and two other experiments in the Denver Art Museum Interpretive Project, Roberts offers only one example to show how the constructivist mode might be implemented: the Wichita Art Museum's

"Visitors' Viewpoints" handouts that affirm visitors' meaning-making processes (Roberts, p. 144). Of course, there must be others; the Wichita model is particularly easy to emulate, and I have seen variations of it in use at the Walker Art Center and in "Visual Thinking Strategies" tours at the High Museum of Art.

14. There may well be other, even more significant examples that are currently unknown to me. I select these two because they happened to cross my rather narrow path, and I apologize for overlooking others that haven't come to my attention.

15. Robert Cohon, "Art 101, Hard Teacher of Curators," *Curator*, September 1997, pp. 173-75. Other specifics about "Discovery and Deceit" can be found in Beverly Serrell, "Paying Attention: The Duration and Allocation of Visitors' Time in Museum Exhibitions," *Curator*, June 1997, pp. 108-25.

16. The exhibition's interpretive goals and devices, it should be noted, do not depend on constructivist theory.

17. Serrell, "Paying Attention," p. 119. Serrell hopes to expand the database with the idea that researchers will eventually be able to identify a "set of common characteristics for successful (or thoroughly used) exhibitions," p. 122.

18. Nancy Parezo, co-curator of the exhibition, has spent 10 years researching Douglas's fashion shows, which she considers one of the most effective outreach programs in the history of American museums. Her book on the subject has been accepted for publication by the Smithsonian Institution Press.

19. Both of the show's curators are used to working cooperatively with members of the American Indian community and like to solicit multiple perspectives in all their decision making. The Denver Art Museum's American Indian Task Force strongly endorsed the plan for "Fashion Pathways."

20. Roberts, p. 143.

MUSEUMS
AND A LEARNING COMMUNITY

by Diane Frankel

I am in a philosophical frame of mind as I sit down to write this article, because I find it so meaningful to be the recipient of the John Cotton Dana Award. As one of the handful of populist museum directors at the turn of the century, Dana had a mission to "promote public education and visual instruction." He understood the important role the museum could play in a community to unite people and reinforce the virtues of citizenship. He knew that museums were educational as well as social places and that they could transmit values. He recognized that they could communicate a great deal to immigrants about what it was to be an American. The relationship of the museum as both an educational institution (with its ability to help humans perceive) and as community resource (with its ability to bring people together) is closer to realization today than ever before. The great strength of our museums is in their evolving relationship to our changing society. Museums today have a much clearer outward focus on visitors and the community.

The role of the museum educator has expanded significantly. The museum educator uses expertise about how people learn and what museums can teach to enrich the visitor's experience. In addition the museum educator has a voice in identifying audiences that the museum is not serving and finding ways to connect with these audiences. And with the welcoming of a new audience, the museum educator has an important role to play in seeing the museum's place in its community evolve.

When I was a child in New York City in the 1950s, I visited museums on Sundays with my father. I was lucky to have a guide who, while he did not know a lot about art, knew that it was important to look carefully and to discuss what you were observing. There was never quite enough information for me, and I can remember being very curious about how to learn more about the variety of objects on display. We visited lots of different types of museums and this inspired a deep and abiding love in me for all kinds of museums. I was comfortable entering the museums with my father because he was obviously at ease. He never doubted that he belonged there and conveyed that comfort to me. My father had come to the United States as an immigrant and enjoyed all the treasures America had to offer. To him, some of the most important treasures were the museums in New York, and he wanted to share them with his children. Sunday afternoons were spent either at the Cloisters, the American Museum of Natural History, the zoo, or one of the many art museums. I still go to museums on Sunday afternoons in whatever city I find myself.

Many years later when I was choosing a career in the museum field, I knew that many people did not feel as comfortable as I did visiting museums on those Sunday afternoons. I wanted to help visitors feel at ease in museums and help them understand more deeply what they were seeing. Becoming a museum educator, therefore, was a very deliberate choice. The role, while a relatively new one in the mid-1970s, was attracting a lot of interest. Fortunately, by 1976 some of today's giants in the field were speaking out, and AAM's Education Committee had come into existence. The early educators inspired the newcomers and provided us with a sense of importance about what we were attempting to accomplish in our own institutions. Today, we take for granted the role of the museum educator as central to the mission of museum, but in the '70s this was hardly the case. My first job after graduating from the museum education program at George Washington University was in an art museum. I definitely felt that my mission was to convince the director and curators about the importance of providing information to visitors—any information.

Many interesting discussions ensued, and I often found myself the lone voice in the museum. Handouts, engaging labels, video, questions, quotations, docents were all part of my arsenal—an arsenal I used strategically so that many of the ideas I offered would gain credence. A handout that engaged visitors with Clyfford Still paintings was removed initially but eventually put back for visitors' use. Another handout was created for an exhibition of works by Picasso, Braque, and Leger. It contained photographs of some of the paintings, including one of a cubist work that had inadvertently been turned upside down. Scores of visitors proclaimed to the staff that the painting was hung upside down. Ah, the power of the printed image.

By the time I left that museum, I felt that I had made a difference—in the way the docents interacted with the public, with the type of in-depth programs provided for school children, and with the written guides provided for adult visitors. But I never felt that I affected the way explanatory labels were presented or what happened on the walls of the galleries. The museum director was from the school that believed that "art spoke for itself," and I never convinced him otherwise. The museum's curators believed that educators should be involved, but after all of the major decisions had been made.

My opportunity to direct a children's museum in the 1980s allowed me to expand my view of the educational role of museums to include the museum's civic role. By then educational research had come a long way in helping those of us engaged in museum education to understand the importance of making educational experiences participatory and interactive. Social research pointed out the numerous issues our cities faced, and children's museums felt responsible for engaging with their community in working toward possible solutions. The children's museums' initial and central focus on the visitors—children and families—went hand in hand with a focus on the community and the social issues that concerned our visitors. Today, for more and more museums of all types that had focused primarily on the object, the emphasis has expanded and now takes into consideration the importance of the visitor. And, as with children's museums, all museums know that when the walls come down to let in more of the community, they also let more of the museum into the community.

Many museums have increasingly identified themselves as educational institutions and have expanded their mission statements to reflect their wealth of educational activities. *Excellence and Equity*, the AAM publication, addressed the need for both excellence and equity at our institutions. Because education is seen as central to the mission, it has become more intertwined with the museum's other functions. While museum educators are playing a more central role in decision making, I do have a concern that when everybody takes responsibility, no one takes responsibility. With educators' expanded role there is a real need for them to be clear about what they want to accomplish. They not only need to be concerned about what is going on within in their galleries and classrooms but outside their walls as well. They have an increasing responsibility to ensure that members of the expanded community feel welcome within the institution. This is a major shift in their roles and it cannot be relegated to what is currently called "outreach." It needs to be embedded in the very philosophy of the museum. The very concept of being an educational institution means not only expanded audiences from pre-school to seniors but also an ethnically diverse audience. Museum educators have taken on this additional and sometimes uncomfortable role—being the conscience of the institution. We increasingly have to ask, Do we serve all of our audiences? How do we make them feel welcome and included? To whom is our institution accessible? If many members of our community do not feel included, what is our responsibility?

When I was a museum educator, I only dimly understood that I had this expanded responsibility because I was working so hard to influence the director and curators about how to make the gallery experience accessible for the casual adult visitor as well as for school groups. But in many areas of the country there is an increasingly diverse audience who might visit our museums if they knew what was available and did not feel uncomfortable or awkward. Giving visitors the tools to fully connect with what the museum has to offer falls within the purview of the museum educator. Community advisory groups can help the museum understand the culture and mores of a community group and can spread the word that the museum is an interesting and friendly environment for individuals and their families.

Research has told us that people come to museums to be educated, entertained, and to enjoy a social time together. These activities are not mutually exclusive and can be enjoyed at the same time. But people who do not think of museums as social places would not consider a family outing to their local museum. The research that is still being used to define museum visitors states that educational attainment is one indicator of whether someone will visit a museum or not. I have not seen recent research that confirms this, but the indicator also needs to be challenged so that if the conclusion is not valid it will not be used as a rationale for why people are not visitors.

At my swearing-in ceremony as director of the Institute of Museum Services (now the Institute of Museum and Library Services), I said that not one institution could afford to remain on the sidelines when so many important issues face our communities. Five years later I would state that even more emphatically than I did in 1993. Museums have a major responsibility to commit themselves to their role as lifelong educational institutions and to contribute to the quality of life in their community. Neither role can be taken lightly, and both present real opportunities and challenges to museums.

Museums that are committed to improving the quality of life in a community must be able to articulate their worth in the community. Museums must make the most of their special power to engage people in creative problem-solving, help people connect, create context for complex issues, open dialogue, and encourage critical thinking. Museums have a unique capacity to place today's issues in context to create a sense of place and a learning community. When this occurs, you have museums that go beyond making people welcome to museums that make communities better. In the past several years, the Institute of Museum and Library Services (IMLS) has given awards for museum community partnerships. Museums have a part to play in their communities by addressing issues and creating better living environments. As relevant, active community partners, museums can build sustainable relationships that address community needs while fulfilling their missions. There are many examples of successful partnerships. A museum that provides a special welcome for senior citizens and uses its collection to evoke memories to help seniors feel connected and to tell their stories. A museum that plays an active role in its community's redevelopment and revitalization, providing an historical context for urban planning and creating a vision for the future. A museum that uses its capacity to create connections and improve esteem to provide after-school programs for middle school children.

I believe so firmly that we must encourage and celebrate museums that play a central role in their communities that I created the IMLS National Award for Museum Service. I worked with Congress to have this award made a part of the Museum and Library Services Act, and I worked with the White House so that the first lady presents the award. Through this initiative museums have received national recognition for being a part of the solution—they help keep children in school and make the streets less mean, keep neighborhoods alive and interesting, help us to appreciate the environment and understand technological advances. These institutions advance our understanding of the richness of our cultural diversity and its potential to make our country great.

Our demographics are changing permanently. Our future audiences will not resemble today's visitors. We have a responsibility to use our museums to their fullest capacity and in the best interest of our communities. Our challenge remains to make our museums' rich educational resources part of everyone's future.

BIOGRAPHIES

BONNIE PITMAN is the executive director of the Bay Area Discovery Museum. She has worked at the University Art Museum and Pacific Film Archive in Berkeley, Seattle Art Museum, New Orleans Museum of Art, and the Winnipeg Gallery in Canada. Pitman has also been a consultant for several television projects and marketing companies.

Pitman has played an active role in the American Association of Museums, serving on the board of directors and as the chair of the task force that wrote the national report, *Excellence and Equity: Education and the Public Dimension of Museums.* She served as chair of the AAM Accreditation Commission and as a member of the commission for 12 years. She is also a member of the council of the Association of Youth Museums and serves on several AYM committees. She has served on advisory committees for the Getty Center for Education in the Arts, the Pew Charitable Trusts, the Association of Science and Technology, and the National Endowment for the Arts, National Endowment for the Humanities, the Institute of Museum and Library Services, and the National Science Foundation. Her awards include the Western Museums Association's Director's Chair Award and the AAM Education Committee's Award for Excellence in Practice in 1983.

SUSAN BERNSTEIN worked at the San Diego Museum of Man for 16 years as education coordinator, developing a docent program, a series of specialized seminars and symposia, many community collaborations, integrated state framework and museum curriculum guides for teachers, and interactive anthropologically themed exhibits for families. Her goal in teaching pre-college and college anthropology is to promote cultural understanding, and she has given classes, workshops, and lectures on this subject. She served on the boards of directors of the Western

Museums Association and the California Association of Museums. Bernstein was the recipient of the AAM Education Committee's Award for Excellence in Practice in 1996.

CAROLYN P. BLACKMON retired from the Field Museum in 1996 after 25 years in the education department. She developed the museum's first volunteer program; introduced adult education courses, performances, and field trips; organized the outreach program for caregivers and children; expanded the loan center for teachers; and established family workshops and overnight events. In 1978 she was promoted to chair of the department and published *Teach the Mind, Touch the Spirit—A Guide to Focused Field Trips* following an extensive teacher training series. Blackmon's interest in training issues encouraged her to develop "Museums: Agents for Public Education," a multi-year program supported by the W. K. Kellogg Foundation that focused on educational strategies, team building, and professional growth for 500 staff members from 300 museums. The project evolved into the publication, *Open Conversations—Strategies for Professional Development in Museums*. Blackmon has served as president of AAM's Education Committee, the Midwest Museum Regional Conference, and the Illinois Association of Museums, as well as in numerous other community and national capacities. In 1992, she received the AAM Education Committee's Award for Excellence in Practice.

TESSA BRIDAL is director of public programs for the Science Museum of Minnesota, where for 14 years she has headed the museum's theater program and, more recently, its science demonstrations. Bridal is also the founder of the annual Theater in Museums Workshop and of AAM's Museum Theater Professional Interest Council. In her capacity as chair of the council, she oversees the publication of *Museum Theater Journal*. She has served as program consultant to museums in the United States and Canada and has published articles in various professional magazines and journals. Bridal recently published her first novel, *The Tree of Red Stars*, winner of the 1997 Milkweed National Prize for Fiction. She received the

AAM Education Committee's Award for Excellence in Practice in 1994.

MARLENE CHAMBERS has been director of publications at the Denver Art Museum since 1974. In that role, she has edited (and often written) everything from exhibition catalogues to lure brochures and gallery labels. With undergraduate majors in education and English and M.A. degrees in English and art history, it's not surprising she has taken more than a passing interest in museum education and looks on the John Cotton Dana Award for Leadership she received from the AAM Education Committee in 1996 as the capstone of her career. Published in such journals as *Comparative Literature*, *Forum*, *Museum News*, *The Exhibitionist*, and *Curator*, her occasional essays explore topics in aesthetics, criticism, and art history, as well as issues of communication and learning in the museum setting.

SALLY DUENSING has spent 25 years at the Exploratorium, working on education programs and numerous exhibit development projects, primarily in the field of perception and cognition, including co-direction of the 1998 exhibition on cultural, biological, cognitive aspects of human memory. As science liaison, Duensing oversees connections between the Exploratorium and the scientific community by developing seminars, lectures, and ways of bringing current scientific research into the public museum environment. She also directs the Exploratorium's Osher Fellowship program in which five outstanding people from the arts, sciences, and humanities serve in residence at the museum. As the Exploratorium's museum liaison to the international museum community, she has created professional development programs for staff from museums around the world. She also has written articles for research journals and informal education books. Duensing received the AAM Education Committee's Award for Excellence in Practice in 1993.

ZORA MARTIN FELTON is chief of education, emerita, Anacostia Museum and Center for African American History and Culture, Smithsonian Institution, Washington, D.C. During her tenure at there, she was dedicated to the substantive involvement of community residents in the work of the museum. Her published works and educational programs and projects have served as models for other museums across the country. She curated the nationally acclaimed exhibition, "The Rat: Man's Invited Affliction" and is the co-author of *A Different Drummer: John R. Kinard and the Anacostia Museum, 1967-1989*. She was the recipient of the African American Museums Association Margaret T. Burroughs Award for Exceptional Contributions in Museum Education in 1989, and the AAM Education Committee's Award for Excellence in Practice in 1991.

DIANE FRANKEL was appointed director of the Institute of Museum Services (now the Institute of Museum and Library Services) by President Clinton in 1993. As director of the institute, Frankel has focused national attention on the roles of museums and libraries in people's lives and the life of the nation. She previously served as executive director of the Bay Area Discovery Museum, located in the Golden Gate National Recreation Area. From 1985 to 1986, she served as dean of the School of Liberal and Professional Arts at the John F. Kennedy University and from 1980 to 1985, as director of the Center for Museum Studies. She also was assistant director of education at the San Francisco Museum of Modern Art from 1976 to 1980, and outreach educator at the University of Botswana, Lesotho, and Swaziland from 1972 to 1973. Frankel received the AAM Education Committee's John Cotton Dana Award for Leadership in 1998.

ALBERTA SEBOLT GEORGE, president of Old Sturbridge Village, joined the museum in 1971 as an experienced educator from the public sector. She came to the museum as director of an E.S.E.A.-Title III program to develop a model teacher training program that would strengthen learning opportunities through collaborative programs between museums and schools. Sebolt George held several management positions, including executive vice president and chief operating officer, prior to becoming the chief executive officer in 1993. She has served as president of the New England Museum Association, vice chair of the board of the American Association of Museums, and chair of a local school committee. She is president of the Worcester County Convention and Visitor Bureau, serves on several advisory boards, and was appointed by President Clinton to the National Museum Services Board of the Institute of Museum and Library Services. Sebolt George received the AAM Education Committee's Award for Excellence in Practice in 1987.

ELAINE HEUMANN GURIAN is currently acting director of the Cranbrook Institute of Art, Bloomfield Hills, Mich. She also serves as an advisor/consultant to museums that are beginning, building, or reinventing themselves. She was director of education, Museum of Contemporary Art, Boston (1969-72), and director, exhibit center (1972-85) and associate director (1985-87) at the Children's Museum of Boston. As deputy assistant secretary for museums at the Smithsonian Institution (1987-90), she oversaw 14 museums and was the lead staff person for the African American Museum Project and the Experimental Gallery. Gurian also served as the deputy director for public program planning at the National Museum of the American Indian (1990-91) and deputy director, U.S. Holocaust Memorial Museum (1991-94). She was the editor of *Institutional Trauma: The Effect of Major Change on Museum Staff*, published by AAM, and received the AAM Education Committee's Award for Excellence in Practice in 1984.

SUSAN BASS MARCUS has been curator of the Paul and Gabriella Rosenbaum ARTiFACT Center at Spertus Museum, Chicago, since 1988, and helped create the center's interactive gallery, including its multi-level archeological dig exhibit. She began her career in museum education at ExpressWays Children's Museum (now the Chicago Children's Museum). There, she was responsible for the design and implementation of several long-term workshops for group tours, family puppet theater programs, and a professional development course targeting classroom teachers. She refined her training with a three-month internship at L'Atelier des enfants, Le Centre Georges Pompidou in Paris, France. During this period, she worked with more than 400 French schoolchildren in museum visual and performing arts programs. Marcus holds two master of arts degrees, the latest in interdisciplinary arts with a practicum in museum education. She was the recipient of the AAM Education Committee's Award for Excellence in Practice in 1995. She is also a professional puppeteer and storyteller.

BARBARA MOORE has served in and led education departments at the Corcoran Gallery of Art and National Gallery of Art over the past 25 years, focusing primarily in the areas of 20th-century art, photography, and 19th-century French and American painting. Issues of aesthetic understanding, the creative process, and the relevance of art to wide-ranging communities and interests are touchstones of her work. She has created interpretive programs for a wide range of exhibitions including "Facing History: the Black Image in American Art 1710-1940" and "L'Amour Fou: Photography and Surrealism," and has published guides and children's books on museum collections, most recently co-authoring *The Nine-Ton Cat: Behind the Scenes at an Art Museum* (Boston: Houghton Mifflin Company, 1997). In her current position as head of education publications for the education division at the National Gallery of Art, Washington, D.C., she writes and oversees the printed and electronic materials produced by the division. She received the AAM Education Committee's Award for Excellence in Practice in 1997.

MARY ELLEN MUNLEY is director of education and outreach at the Field Museum, Chicago. She oversees all aspects of the department, including public programs, school programs, performing arts, educational media, community partnerships, and special projects. Munley has more than 15 years of experience as a museum educator and audience research and evaluation specialist. Prior to joining the Field Museum in January 1997, she was chief of museum education at the New York State Education Department and the New York State Museum. She is the author of several articles and presentations and recently ended a four-year term as chair of EdCom. She also contributed to AAM's *Museums for a New Century: A Report of the Commission on Museums for a New Century* and *Excellence and Equity: Education and the Public Dimension of Museums*. Munley received the AAM Education Committee's Award for Excellence in Practice in 1998.

DANIELLE RICE is senior curator of education at the Philadelphia Museum of Art. Before becoming curator of education at the Philadelphia Museum of Art in 1986, Rice headed the education departments of the Wadsworth Atheneum in Hartford, Conn., and the National Gallery of Art in Washington, D.C. Rice has received numerous awards including the AAM Education Committee's Award for Excellence in Practice in 1988 and the Pennsylvania Art Education Association's Museum Educator of the Year Award in 1996.

MICHAEL SPOCK works as a consultant to museums and funders and is based at the Chapin Hall Center for Children at the University of Chicago, where he is conducting research on learning in museums and other informal settings. From 1986 to 1994, he served as vice president for public programs at the Field Museum, Chicago. Prior to going to the Field, he was director of the Boston Children's Museum for 23 years and before that designed and produced exhibits for the Ohio State Museum and the Dayton Museum of Natural History. In addition to the AAM Education Committee's John Cotton Dana Award, which he received in 1988, Spock has received the AAM's Distinguished Service Award and the Association of Youth Museum's Great Friend to Kids Award.

JUDITH WHITE has been active in museum education for more than 25 years. She worked at the Children's Museum in Boston, assembled the first Discovery Room at the Smithsonian Institution's National Museum of Natural History in Washington, D.C., and was in charge of education at the Smithsonian's National Zoo for approximately 20 years. She has been principal investigator for two National Science Foundation projects, both in cooperation with several other zoos. White is past president of the International Association of Zoo Educators and received the AAM Education Committee's Award for Excellence in Practice in 1989. She currently lives in northern California, where she works as a consultant to the Exploratorium, San Francisco; the National Science Resources Center in Washington, D.C.; and other organizations.

PATTERSON B. WILLIAMS has been an art museum educator since 1966, working at the Walters Art Gallery, Philadelphia Museum of Art, and Denver Museum of Art, where she is now the master teacher for Asian art and the dean of the education department. In over 30 years of teaching with art museum collections she has steadily pursued various means of helping visitors to have personally rewarding experiences with artworks in museum galleries. At that mid-career point where some decide to step into museum administration, Williams decided to remain focused on museum education and to attempt to incorporate more direct teaching into her work. Currently, two types of teaching intrigue her most—developing interpretive installations that help visitors explore the human context that created the artwork displayed and working directly with children to help them explore and love the varied art and cultures of the world. She was the recipient of the AAM Education Committee's Award for Excellence in Practice in 1990.

INDEX